THE VATICAN
AND CHRISTIAN ROME

CITTÀ DEL VATICANO

With ecclesiastical approval

Lectori salutem! *We greet you in the ancient language of Rome and in the venerable language of the Catholic Church. We repeat: Greetings to you the reader! Whoever you are, from wherever you come, whether pilgrim or tourist or simply observer, the Vatican and Christian Rome welcome you and extend their greetings to you as a brother or sister and as a friend.*

The Vatican and Christian Rome have been inseparably united in the person of Peter and his successor, the Pope, who is the visible head of the universal Church and the bishop of the Eternal City. This guidebook comments not only upon the history and the art of the Vatican and Christian Rome but also upon its mission. This mission is spiritual: while it provides the ultimate and profound explanation of an occurrence enduring now two thousand years and of the works of art produced and collected in the course of centuries, it also continues to develop and renew itself for the benefit of all men.

May you see in these pages the eloquent and admirable witness to man's initiative and genius as well as the continuity and relevance of a message that is always living, transcending space and time and having its origin in the Absolute.

Chapter One

THE
VATICAN:
CITY
OF THE
SPIRIT

The visitor to the Vatican feels a strong desire to understand fully what he sees. Archaeologists, historians, artists and men of letters have recounted and explained the history of its monuments; but something of far greater significance still remains to be added, something that can escape the analysis of the experts: its living history, that which makes the Vatican the city of the spirit. The person who fails to perceive the spiritual side of the Vatican, that is to say, its real life, finds no adequate explanation for it. Understanding this reality means having an exact idea of why this centre of spiritual values has been enriched with the highest forms of art. The artistic treasures of the Vatican exist in relation to a higher idea.

The visitor arriving for the first time in this universal city of the spirit immediately feels the stimulus of countless memories crowding the mind at every turn. Entering Saint Peter's, visiting the Museums, walking along a loggia or crossing a courtyard, one is immersed in the history of times both ancient and modern and feels their evocative force. One pictures what this place was once like, beside the *Via Triumphalis,* on the edge of the city of Rome. The *Ager Vaticanus,* as it was then called, a hilly area without great fertility or beauty situated outside the fourth century B.C. Servian Walls, became a Christian holy place between the years 64 and 67 A.D. It was here that a cross was erected on which the Apostle Peter, the first Pope and Bishop of Rome, was crucified, head downwards, in accordance with his wish.

His venerated body was buried not far from the spot where he was martyred. Later the Constantinian Basilica was built there, a great church with a nave and four side aisles. Invading Goths, Vandals and Saracens came, but in spite of being damaged and sacked the Basilica remained standing. In the centuries before and after the year 1000, throngs of pilgrims—the " Romei " as they were called—flocked here to honour the tomb of the Prince of the Apostles. Often they climbed on their knees the thirty-five steps leading up to the square portico. More than thirty Popes were buried in that portico, which was called " Il Paradiso ". *O Roma Nobilis* was the hymn that the faithful sang as soon as the City came into view, and they paid homage to the Christian faith by their devout visits to the Basilica. There emperors and kings were crowned by the Pope before the tomb of Saint Peter, the fisherman from Galilee. Finally, in the sixteenth century, the new Basilica was built, the one that is still today the goal of pilgrims and visitors, in an unbroken history of universal attraction. What is the basic reason for its constant appeal?

The Church and the Successor of Saint Peter

The Vatican is the residence of the Roman Pontiff, the visible head of the Church founded by Jesus Christ. This is the central fact about which all others revolve.

The Church is a spiritual fellowship and at the same time a visible society. She is made up of those who have received

Perugino: Jesus giving the Keys to St Peter (Sistine Chapel)

baptism, hold the one same faith in Christ, profess the same teaching and the same acceptance of the Word of God, recognize seven sacraments and receive them as means of grace, and accept the pastoral service of the successors of Saint Peter and the Apostles. The Church is open to all: she prays and works that there may be one fold and one Shepherd. Her essential marks are four. The Church is *one:* she lives in the unity of faith, of worship paid to God, of Eucharistic celebration, and of sacramental life; she finds unity through the Roman Pontiff. The Church is *holy:* this is so because her Founder is holy and because all her members are called to holiness, because she has the Holy Spirit's assistance, because of her teaching, and because of the great number of her members who have been virtuous to the point of heroism and have been declared saints. The Church is *catholic:* she was not founded for the benefit of one people or nation but for the whole of mankind, because all men are called to become God's people. The Church is *apostolic:* she is founded on the Apostles, with Saint Peter at their head, and on their successors, the Pope and the bishops united with him.

The Church continues the work of redemption and salvation willed by the Blessed Trinity and achieved by Jesus Christ, the Son of God who became man through the virginal motherhood of Blessed Mary. For this reason Jesus has entrusted the Pope, the bishops and the priests with spiritual powers to enable them to serve their brothers and sisters. These powers are those of teaching with authority, of governing, and of administering the sacraments: a God-given mission of truth and love for the benefit of all mankind. Faithful to the teachings of the Gospel, the Church also brings a message of equality and brotherhood, of justice and peace, of complete human development, both personal and collective.

The Pope's teaching, which guarantees the common faith, is imparted by means of discourses, messages, encyclicals, apostolic letters, etc., and at times by means of definitions endowed with doctrinal infallibility. He possesses the fullness of legislative power, which is exercised by the issuing of apostolic constitutions, " motu proprio's ", etc. He also has full judicial and administrative power over the whole Church.

Roman Pontiff, Pope, Supreme Pontiff, Vicar of Christ, Holy Father, His Holiness—these are titles that designate the Successor of Peter. " Papa ", the Latin word from which " pope " is derived, is an affectionate form of the word *pater* (father). It was once used for all bishops, but in the sixth century it began to be reserved to the Pope. In certain important documents the Bishop of Rome calls himself *Servus servorum Dei,* servant of the servants of God.

The Pope and the Bishops

Within the Catholic Church two rites are distinguished: the Eastern and the Latin. These are divided into numerous local Churches, which are entrusted to the care of the bishops. The Pope is the head of the episcopal college. He maintains close contact with the bishops throughout the world (there were more than 3000 in 1973). He can convene them in an **ecumenical council** under his presidency, to discuss with them important questions concerning the life of the whole Church. The most recent of the twenty-one ecumenical councils held in the course of the twenty centuries of the Church's history was the Second Vatican Council, so called because it was held in Saint Peter's Basilica in the Vatican, as was the First Vatican Council of 1869-1870. The Second Vatican Council was inaugurated by John XXIII in 1962 and solemnly closed by Paul VI three years later.

In 1965, during the last session of the Second Vatican Council, Paul VI instituted a new form of organic collaboration between Pope and bishops: the **Synod of Bishops,** presided over by the Bishop of Rome himself. The Synod has already met several times to discuss collegially matters of interest for the universal Church. The agenda is determined by the Pope, often on the basis of proposals made by the episcopate. Its function is normally a consultative one. The General Secretariat is situated at Piazza Pio XII, 3, the square linking Saint Peter's Square and Via della Conciliazione.

Since 1967 diocesan bishops have been included with cardinals as members of the departments of the Roman Curia.

The College of Cardinals

In exercising his mission of Supreme Pastor of the entire Church, the Pope is assisted directly by the cardinals and by the departments of the Roman Curia.

The cardinals—the word derives from *cardo* (hinge), a term expressing stability and belonging—are the electors and the chief advisers of the Pope. The election of the Pope has been reserved to them since 1179. For this purpose they meet in **conclave,** a word meaning " an assembly behind locked doors ". The right of a cardinal to enter the conclave ceases, in accordance with a recent decree of Pope Paul VI, when he reaches the age of eighty.

For almost four centuries, from 1586 onwards, the number of cardinals was fixed at a maximum of seventy, but the Church's expansion caused John XXIII and Paul VI to increase their number and make them more representative.

A centuries-old tradition is that of holding **consistories.** These are meetings of the cardinals convened for some solemn act on the part of the visible head of the Church. It is the Pope's custom to receive the Sacred College on other occasions too. At the presentation of Christmas greetings and on his feast day, he customarily addresses to them a discourse on the state of the Church in the world and on the most serious problems facing mankind in the religious and social fields.

By ancient tradition the cardinals are divided into three orders: bishops, priests and deacons. In 1962, John XXIII decreed that anyone named a cardinal who was not yet a bishop would receive episcopal ordination.

Few cardinals live in Vatican City. The office held by the

Cardinal Secretary of State, however, requires that he should reside in the Apostolic Palace, since he is the principal and closest collaborator of the Pope.

Cardinals belong to departments of the Roman Curia either as prefects or as members.

The Roman Curia

The Roman Curia is a body made up of a number of departments that assist the Pope in his office of chief Pastor of the universal Church. Among the designations of this office is the name " Holy See " or " Apostolic See ", terms which are also applied to the Curia.

The present form of the Roman Curia was established by Paul VI's apostolic constitution *Regimini Ecclesiae Universae* of 15 August 1967. The heads of departments, members (cardinals and bishops), secretaries and consultors are named by the Pope for a five-year period. The appointment is renewable. Provision is made for closer contacts between the departments of the Roman Curia and the bishops and the episcopal conferences.

Under its new form and as a result of the selection of personnel from many different countries, the Roman Curia has more clearly assumed an international aspect.

1. In the apostolic constitution of 1967 mentioned above, first place is given to two offices working more directly with the Pope. These are the **Secretariat of State** and the **Council for the Public Affairs of the Church** and they are situated, close to the Pope's apartments, on the Third Loggia of the Apostolic Palace, the top floor overlooking the Cortile di San Damaso.

The Secretariat of State is the central office for carrying out the Pope's instructions. It is presided over by the Cardinal Secretary of State, who is assisted by the Substitute of the Secretariat of State. It maintains relations with the departments of the Curia, with the episcopate, with the representatives of the Holy See in the various countries, with Governments and their envoys and with private persons. From time to time the Cardinal Secretary of State calls meetings of the cardinals in charge of departments; at these meetings he presides.

In the Secretariat of State are also the management and editorial offices of the *Acta Apostolicae Sedis* (the Holy See's official gazette) and of the *Annuario Pontificio* (The Papal Yearbook). The Secretariat of State also produces an annual publication entitled *L'attività della Santa Sede* (The Activity of the Holy See).

The Council for the Public Affairs of the Church has since 1967 acquired greater autonomy vis-à-vis the Secretariat of State. Previously it formed part of the Secretariat as its First Section, with the title of *Sacred Congregation for the Extraordinary Affairs of the Church.* The Cardinal Secretary of State is its Prefect, thereby ensuring unity of action by the two offices. The Council for the Public Affairs has its own Secretary and deals with matters concerning negotiations with States and diplomatic relations with nations; jointly with the Secretariat of State it deals with matters involving the missions of the papal representatives.

In the field of international law the Holy See possesses the prerogative of sovereignty, distinct from the territorial sovereignty of Vatican City State: it represents throughout the world the Catholic Church, which is a society independent of any earthly power. As a sovereign entity it has long enjoyed the right of active and passive legation: it sends out representatives and receives those of States. These diplomatic relations have considerably developed in recent years.

At the beginning of 1973 the Holy See had seventy-five representatives of a diplomatic character (apostolic nuncios and pro-nuncios) and fourteen non-diplomatic representatives (apostolic delegates). The Holy See's diplomatic personnel receive their training in a long-established school set up for this purpose, the **Pontifical Ecclesiastical Academy.** The diplomatic corps accredited to the Holy See is composed of seventy-eight missions (embassies and legations). As a general rule the envoys reside in the city of Rome, where they enjoy normal diplomatic immunity. It is not possible for them to live in the Vatican itself because of the restricted size of its territory.

The tasks of the Papal Representatives are defined in Paul VI's " motu proprio " *Sollicitudo Omnium Ecclesiarum* of 24 June 1969. The Holy See's envoy, who is usually an archbishop, has, first of all, ecclesial functions. In other words he is at the service of the local Churches and acts as a link between them and the Pope. In addition to this primary mission, he also acts as the representative of the Holy See to the State and government to which he is accredited, in order to advance the cause of peace and progress of peoples.

The Holy See is sensitive to the problems of peace, disarmament, international security and development, as well as to the social, cultural, and scientific problems of the modern world. It therefore also has permanent representatives at international organizations (UNO, and some of its specialized agencies such as UNESCO, FAO, UNIDO, WHO, ILO, etc.) and at international

The junction of Via della Conciliazione and Piazza Pio XII,
showing the buildings housing the Congregations
of the Roman Curia

non-governmental organizations (such as the International Committee of Historical Sciences, the International Committee of Palaeography, the International Committee for the Neutrality of Medicine, etc.).

2. The *Sacred Congregations* are the Pope's ministries. The name comes from the traditional term " congregation " denoting a ·meeting of the cardinals and bishops who are members of a department. The Congregations are now ten in number. The

document *Regimini Ecclesiae Universae* changed the names of several of them to ones corresponding better to their field of competence or expressing their function more clearly. New needs, especially of a pastoral character, have also necessitated modifications in the structure of the individual departments.

The Congregation of the Holy Office, set up in 1542, was the first to be reformed. The reform was effected by the " motu proprio " *Integrae Servandae* of 7 December 1965. In conformity with the principle that " the defence of the faith is now best

The Holy Office building,
which houses the Sacred Congregation
for the Doctrine of the Faith

provided for by the advancement of doctrine ", this department has assumed the name of the **Sacred Congregation for the Doctrine of the Faith.** Its field of competence covers all questions concerning faith and morals or matters pertaining thereto. Its consultors are chosen from among the theologians of the whole Catholic world. On 11 April 1969, an **International Theological Commission** was set up within the Sacred Congregation for the Doctrine of the Faith. It is composed of thirty representatives of various schools and nations, and meets at least once a year. Linked to the Congregation is the **Pontifical Biblical Commission,** which was reorganized by Paul VI in 1971.

The offices of the Congregation for the Doctrine of the Faith are in the Holy Office Building, situated in Piazza del Sant'Uffizio, beyond the colonnade of Saint Peter's Square. Almost all the other congregations are in two buildings in Piazza Pio XII, which links Saint Peter's Square with Via della Conciliazione.

The **Sacred Congregation for Bishops,** previously called the Consistorial Congregation, was founded in 1588. In has competence regarding the local Churches and their pastors in all countries not entrusted to the Sacred Congregations for the Eastern Churches and for the Evangelization of Peoples. The Congregation is at the service of the bishops and concerns itself with the establishment and territorial modification of dioceses. It provides for the nomination of bishops, and takes an interest in their pastoral activity and the state of their dioceses. It also follows the development of provincial councils (that is to say, those of ecclesiastical provinces, each of which is made up of several dioceses within a single nation) and studies the proceedings of national episcopal conferences. It arranges in advance matters to be dealt with In consistories. Two pontifical commissions have been linked with it: the **Pontifical Commission for Latin America** and the **Pontifical Commission for the Pastoral Care of Migrant and Itinerant People** (tourists, nomads, seamen, etc.).

The **Sacred Congregation for the Eastern Churches** dates from 1862. At that time it was linked with the Congregation *de Propaganda Fide,* but it became independent in 1917. It exercises in relation to the dioceses, bishops, clergy, religious and laity of Eastern rite all the faculties that the Congregations for Bishops, for the Clergy, for Religious and Secular Institutes, and for Catholic Education possess for the same classes of persons of Latin rite. It has exclusive competence for some countries of Africa and the Middle East. Its offices are in the Palazzo dei Convertendi, Via della Conciliazione, 34.

The **Sacred Congregation for the Discipline of the Sacraments,** set up in 1908, concerns itself with everything touching the discipline of all seven sacraments—Baptism, Confirmation, the Eucharist, Penance or Confession, Holy Orders, Matrimony and the Anointing of the Sick—leaving intact the prerogatives of other departments with regard to doctrine, ritual and marriage cases.

The **Sacred Congregation for the Clergy** dates back to the one established in 1564 to supervise the correct interpretation and observance of the regulations sanctioned by the Council of Trent. Hence its historical name of the *Sacred Congregation of the Council,* which was used until 1967, long after the department's competence in that field had ceased. The Congregation is at the service of the clergy; it fosters programmes connected with priests' spirituality and with pastoral renewal. It reviews the forms of priests' apostolates and works for the better distri-

17

The Propaganda building in Piazza di Spagna,
the headquarters of the Sacred Congregation for the Evangelization of Peoples,
also known as de Propaganda Fide

bution of the clergy in the various countries of the world. It concerns itself with all matters connected with the preaching of the word of God and catechetical activities. It is competent in the field of preserving and administering the temporal goods of the Church, including its artistic heritage.

The **Sacred Congregation for Religious and Secular Institutes,** called the *Congregation of Regulars* from 1586 to 1908 and of *Religious* from 1908 to 1967, has competence with regard to " religious life " (the profession of the evangelical counsels by means of the vows of poverty, chastity and obedience, and of the common life in orders and congregations of men and women), as well as with regard to secular institutes, a newer form of the practice of the evangelical counsels.

The **Sacred Congregation for the Evangelization of Peoples,** which keeps as an alternative title its historical name of *de Propaganda Fide,* and which is situated in a building of the same name in Piazza di Spagna, was set up in 1622 for the purpose of preaching the faith in the mission countries. It carried out a wide-ranging activity, principally in the newly-discovered lands but also in the countries of Europe that had been removed from the profession of the Catholic faith. It now concerns itself with many aspects of the life of the Church in certains areas of Europe and the Americas, in almost the whole of Africa, in the Far East, Australia, New Zealand and Oceania, with the exception of practically the whole of the Philippines.

The **Sacred Congregation for Divine Worship** and the **Sacred Congregation for the Causes of the Saints** derive from the previously existing *Congregation of Rites* and were set up by the apostolic constitution *Sacra Rituum Congregatio* of 8 May 1969. The first named is competent in all matters regarding divine worship—liturgical or extra-liturgical—in the Churches of Latin rite. The second concerns itself with the procedures whereby members of the Church who have practised in a heroic degree the Christian virtues (faith, hope, charity, prudence, justice, fortitude, temperance, etc.) are proclaimed Blessed or Saints and are thus held up to the faithful for veneration and imitation. These procedures are called " beatification " and " canonization ".

The **Sacred Congregation for Catholic Education** (formerly that of *Seminaries and Universities*) has competence over seminaries for young men aspiring to the priesthood as members of the diocesan clergy. It also has competence over houses of formation of religious and secular institutes in regard to the cultural preparation of their students. It likewise supervises all universities, faculties, institutes and higher schools of ecclesiastical or civil studies dependent on ecclesiastical authorities,

The Chancery building in Corso Vittorio Emanuele,
which houses the Sacred Roman Rota
and other offices of the Holy See

and all pre-university educational institutes and schools of every type and level depending on ecclesiastical authorities and providing for the education of lay youth.

3. Three Tribunals form part of the Roman Curia:

The **Sacred Apostolic Penitentiary** (Palazzo dei Convertendi, Via della Conciliazione, 34) is competent for cases of conscience in the internal forum, even if not sacramental (outside the sacrament of Penance), and for questions of the discipline of indulgences (remission of the temporal punishment due for sins which have already been forgiven).

The **Supreme Tribunal of the Apostolic Signatura** is the highest jurisdictional body for the resolution of ecclesiastical judicial controversies and for safeguarding law in the administrative order.

The **Sacred Roman Rota** is essentially a tribunal of appeal (but in some cases also a tribunal of first instance), principally for cases of nullity of marriage introduced for the purpose of determining the original invalidity of an apparently valid marriage.

The Signatura and the Rota are situated in Palazzo della Cancelleria Apostolica, Piazza della Cancelleria, 1, Rome.

The building in Piazza San Calisto in the Trastevere district, which houses a number of Secretariats and other offices of the Roman Curia

4. The Second Vatican Council also made it necessary to bring the Roman Curia up to date through the creation of new bodies.

The **Secretariat for Promoting Christian Unity,** situated in Via dell'Erba, 1, not far from Saint Peter's Square, expresses and brings to realization the Holy See's commitment to ecumenism, which is aimed at the restoration of unity between all believers in Christ. Relations of a religious character with Jews come within its competence.

The **Secretariat for Non-Christians** has for its purpose dialogue with non-Christian religious confessions (Moslems, Buddhists, Hindus, etc.) which have outstanding spiritual and moral values. It seeks to foster human solidarity in a spirit of universal brotherhood.

The **Secretariat for Non-Believers** has the aim of studying present-day atheism in its various forms and of advancing dialogue with sincere non-believers.

The **Council for the Laity** and the **Pontifical Commission Justice and Peace** were set up on 6 January 1967. Their members are mainly lay people. The Council concerns itself with the function of the laity in the Church, with collaboration by the faithful with the hierarchy, and with the various movements of the lay apostolate. The Commission's aim is to advance the development of poor countries and to foster peace and social justice between nations. It has a number of study committees.

The four last-mentioned bodies have their offices in the Trastevere district of Rome, at Piazza San Calisto, 16.

5. The Pope is also assisted in the fulfilment of his mission as visible head of the universal Church by certain other **Pontifical Commissions,** such as those **for Social Communications** (press, radio, television, cinema), **for the Revision of the Code of Canon Law, for the Revision of the Code of Eastern Canon Law, for the Interpretation of the Decrees of the Second Vatican Council,** etc.

The **Pontifical Council " Cor Unum ",** set up by Paul VI in 1971, has for its aim the coordination of the relief and charitable activities of the Church with a view to contributing more effectively to human advancement and social development in needy countries.

The **Committee for the Family,** established by Pope Paul VI in 1973, has the task of studying the spiritual, moral and social problems of the family within a spiritual context.

The **Holy Father's Relief Service,** directed by the Almoner of His Holiness, runs numerous charitable works for the benefit of needy persons who turn to the Pope for assistance.

6. The Roman Curia also includes certain *Offices:*

The **Apostolic Camera** (Palazzo San Carlo, Vatican City) has charge of and administers the temporal goods and rights of the Holy See when it is vacant, that is from the death of a pope until the election of his successor.

The **Prefecture of the Economic Affairs of the Holy See** (Palazzo delle Congregazioni, Largo del Colonnato, 3, Rome), set up in 1967 by the already mentioned apostolic constitution of Paul VI, *Regimini Ecclesiae Universae,* has the task of coordinating and supervising the administration of the Holy See's property.

The **Administration of the Patrimony of the Apostolic See** (located in the Apostolic Palace of the Vatican) administers the greater part of the properties and financial resources that the Holy See needs for the performance of its service as the central government of the Church and for its mission in the world.

The **Prefecture of the Papal Household** combines the functions formerly carried out by the Congregation for Ceremonies, the Major-domo and the Maestro di Camera of His Holiness. It prepares audiences and papal ceremonies (except for the strictly liturgical part), makes arrangements for the Pope's visits inside Rome, and collaborates with the Secretariat of State in preparing his journeys abroad.

The **Office for Papal Ceremonies,** according to norms approved by Paul VI on 1 January 1970, concerns itself with papal liturgical ceremonies.

The **Central Statistics Office of the Church,** which for the present is part of the Secretariat of State, has the task of collecting and systematizing the data necessary or useful for a better knowledge of the Church's situation. It thus provides pastors with a valuable aid for their apostolate.

The Vatican as a Centre of Culture, Science and Art

In 1960 the entire territory of the Vatican was inscribed in the " International Register of Cultural Works under Special Protection in Case of Armed Conflict ". This was the official recognition of a very special situation, unique in the world. It is not a question of individual parts or monuments; the whole of the Vatican witnesses to and serves the highest spiritual values.

There is a permanent supervisory commission for safeguarding the historical and artistic monuments of the Holy See.

The **Apostolic Library of the Vatican** is famous for its collection of codices and manuscripts of great historical and cultural interest. The idea of a library was conceived by Nicholas V (1447-1455), but it was actually established only after his death, in the year 1475. It now has about 60,000 manuscript volumes, 100,000 manuscript documents, 700,000 printed books and 100,000 engravings and maps. Dependent on the Library are the **Numismatic Cabinet,** which contains the most extensive collection of papal coins and one of the major collections of Roman coins of the time of the Republic, and the **Print and Design Room.** Connected with the Library is the School of Library Science.

About the year 1600 it was suggested that the Holy See should have, in addition to a library, its own central archives. The idea was put into practice under Pius V in the years 1611-1614, and copies of papal bulls dating from the thirteenth century onwards formed the first nucleus. From this beginning derive the present **Secret Archives of the Vatican,** which in the course of the centuries have also incorporated other archives of the various congregations of the Holy See and of some nunciatures. By decree of Leo XIII (1878-1903) the Archives were opened to

The Papal Villa at Castelgandolfo:
the Vatican Observatory

scholars in 1881 and thus became a world centre for historical research. Connected with the Archives is a School for Archivists. In the Vatican there is also a School of Palaeography and Diplomatics.

In the field of the experimental sciences and mathematics the Vatican has an institute of worldwide prestige: the **Pontifical Academy of Sciences,** founded in 1936 by Pius XI (1922-1939). Its origins go back to the ancient Academy of the Lincei, founded in Rome in 1603. Consisting of seventy scholars chosen by the Pope from among the most noted scientists of every nation, it

*The Palazzina of Leo XIII in the Vatican Gardens,
which houses the headquarters of Vatican Radio,
a number of studios and technical installations*

has the goal of fostering science, guaranteeing its freedom and promoting the research essential for the progress of the applied sciences. The seat of the Academy is the Casina of Pius IV in the Vatican Gardens.

An astronomical observatory (originally called the *Pontifical Astronomical Observatory* and in 1797 renamed the **Pontifical**

Vatican Observatory) was set up in the Tower of the Winds, built between 1578 and 1580 by order of Gregory XIII (1572-1585). The reform of the calendar by this Pope in 1582 is connected with this first Observatory; meetings of astronomers were held here. The Observatory was later moved to the summer villa of Leo XIII, not far from the Tower, and finally, under Pius XI, transferred to the papal villa at Castelgandolfo. At this time the Observatory was equipped with modern instruments, and a laboratory of astrophysics was added. The Observatory carries out a systematic programme of observation and research in conjunction with observatories in other parts of the world.

The artistic monuments and the museums will be discussed at greater length in the following chapters, but it may be noted here that there is a special administrative office which has charge of Saint Peter's Basilica: the **Reverenda Fabbrica di San Pietro,** dating from the sixteenth century when the building of the present Basilica was begun. The *Fabbrica* is directed by the Cardinal Archpriest of the Basilica and has architects and technicians among its members. Its workers are called " sampietrini ". There is a **Mosaic Studio** connected with it.

The Vatican has a printing-press, the **Vatican Polyglot Press,** which carries out work in many languages, and a **publishing house.** It has a daily newspaper, **L'Osservatore Romano,** which reports religious and political news and which was founded in 1861. In the official part, which is generally to be found on the first page, *L'Osservatore Romano* prints the Pope's addresses, official documents and news about the Holy See. For the rest, it is a journal of documentation and information about ecclesiastical affairs (with special emphasis on the activity of the Holy See, the life of the Church in the world and contemporary religious problems) and, on an international level, about political, social, cultural and economic matters. There are also weekly editions in English, French, Spanish, Portuguese, German and Italian. Another periodical published by the Vatican is **L'Osservatore della Domenica,** an illustrated weekly founded in 1934. For these daily and weekly publications there is a special printing-press, that of *L'Osservatore Romano.*

Since 1931 the Holy See has had a radio station. Inaugurated

Plan of Vatican City State

by Pius XI and Guglielmo Marconi, **Vatican Radio** now broadcasts in more than thirty languages for a total of about twenty hours a day. It brings even to distant countries the words of the Pope and educational and informative programmes on the Church and its life in the world.

At the end of Via della Conciliazione, before it meets Piazza Pio XII, is located the **Press Service of the Holy See,** where journalists accredited by newspapers in all parts of the world gather for the communication of news and documents.

The Vatican is also a State

The Vatican is also a State: the **State of Vatican City,** in virtue of the Lateran Treaty of 11 February 1929 between the Holy See and Italy. It has a territory of 0.44 square kilometres (about 140 times smaller than that of the Republic of San Marino) and a few hundred inhabitants. Its boundaries are the Colonnade of Saint Peter's Square, Via di Porta Angelica, Piazza del Risorgimento, Via Leone IV, Viale Vaticano, Via della Stazione Vaticana and Via della Sagrestia. As a small remnant of what had been in centuries past—up to 1870—the Papal States, it has the essential and exclusive purpose of providing the See of Peter with the territory necessary to guarantee the liberty of its spiritual mission.

By virtue of the above-mentioned Treaty, certain properties of the Holy See located in Rome enjoy extra-territoriality: the Major Basilicas of Saint John Lateran, Saint Paul Outside-the-Walls and Saint Mary Major; the Catacombs, the buildings housing the Congregations of the Roman Curia and some Colleges and Seminaries. The Papal Villa at Castelgandolfo also enjoys the same privilege.

The Pope is the **head** of Vatican City State. He has full legislative, executive and judicial powers. The first two powers are exercised by a **Pontifical Commission** consisting of cardinals and a lay Special Delegate; the third is exercised by appropriate

The Flag of Vatican City State

Tribunals. In dependence upon the Pontifical Commission, the **Governorate** manages most of the activities of the State through a General Secretariat consisting of seven offices (general affairs, legal affairs, personnel, central accounting, post and telegraph, merchandise, security) and eight General Directorates (for the pontifical monuments, museums and galleries; technical services; Vatican Radio; economic services; Vatican Observatory; health services; archaeological studies and research; the papal villas). On 29 June 1969 a **Board of Consultors** was established to assist the Governorate.

Under the Governorate comes the **Information Office for Pilgrims and Tourists,** located in Saint Peter's Square near the Arch of the Bells. Its principal purpose is to facilitate visits to the Vatican in its religious and cultural aspects.

The State has its own flag. It is divided vertically into two fields: a yellow one next to the staff, and a white one charged with a tiara and two crossed keys.

The State anthem is the " Papal March ", composed by Charles Gounod for the jubilee Mass in honour of the fiftieth anniversary of Pius IX's ordination to the priesthood.

The disbanding of the papal armed corps (the Guard of Honour, the Papal Gendarmes and the Palatine Guard), ordered by Paul VI

Swiss Guards
at the swearing-in ceremony

Bird's-eye view of the buildings of Vatican City State. 1. The Audience Hall - 2. The Holy Office building - 3. The Hospice of Santa Marta - 4. Seat of the Tribunal of Vatican City State and residence of the Vatican Penitentiaries - 5. The Residence of the Canons of St Peter's - 6. The Teutonic College - 7. St Peter's Square - 8. The Ethiopian College - 9. The Governorate - 10. St Peter's Basilica - 11. The Palazzina of Leo XIII - 12. The Casina of Pius IV - 13. The Sistine Chapel - 14. The Courtyard of St Damasus - 15. The Apostolic Palace - 16. The Belvedere Courtyard, Apostolic Vatican Library and part of the Vatican Museums - 17. The Courtyard of the Pine-cone and part of the Vatican Museums - 18. The Vatican Picture Gallery

2 - E

View of the Vatican Gardens

on 14 September 1970, was aimed at emphasizing, even in outward appearances, the religious nature of the mission of Peter's successor. The only corps remaining is that of the **Swiss Guards,** who wear the picturesque uniform said to have been designed by Michelangelo.

A civilian security force, dependent on the Central Office of Security, carries out the necessary functions connected with maintaining order.

The State of Vatican City has its own **postal and· telegraph** services and issues its own stamps. It has its own **coinage,** which circulates freely in Italy. It also has a **railway station.**

*Façade of the Casina of Pius IV
in the Vatican Gardens*

The State is a full member of some international governmental organizations (the Universal Postal Union, the International Union for Telecommunications and the Union for the Protection of Literary and Artistic Works) and also of some that are non-governmental (the International Institute for Administrative Sciences, the World Medical Association).

The architectural nucleus of the City-State consists of Saint Peter's Basilica, the Apostolic Palace, which is built around the Cortile di San Damaso, and the Museums and the Library, within which are the Cortile della Pigna and the Cortile del Belvedere. Numerous Popes have added other buildings, for example the

Palace of the Governorate, which houses the offices of the services mentioned earlier. An important addition has been made in the pontificate of Paul VI: the Audience Hall, designed and built by the architect Pier Luigi Nervi.

To the northwest of the building complex are the Vatican Gardens, situated within the walls built by Paul III, Pius IV and Urban VIII between 1550 and 1640 to extend and to defend the city. These walls are intersected by a part of the walls of the Leonine City.

Within the gardens are the Leonine Tower, named after Leo IV (847-855), who founded the Leonine City, the Casina of Pius IV, the Summer Villa of Leo XIII, a reproduction of the Grotto at Lourdes, presented by the Catholics of France to Leo XIII (1878-1903), and the little chapel of the Madonna della Guardia, built by Benedict XV (1914-1922) to recall the famous shrine of the same name near Genoa.

The most important of the above buildings is the elegant Casina of Pius IV, which now houses the Pontifical Academy of Sciences. It was designed by Pirro Ligorio, and is a masterpiece of harmony of proportion and beauty of composition.

In the centre of the gardens, standing on a tall cylindrical base, is a large statue of the Apostle Peter, the work of Filippo Gnaccorini.

John XXIII had the Tower of Saint John restored, and used to like to go there for short periods before his death. Patriarch Athenagoras of Constantinople stayed there in 1969 during his visit to Paul VI, as did Patriarch Vasken I, Catholicos of All the Armenians, in 1970, and Cardinal Mindszenty of Hungary in 1971.

Various fountains adorn the gardens. Notable among them are the Fountain of the Eagle, or of the Rock, with its figures of dragons and tritons, dominated by a great stone eagle, and the Fountain of the Sacrament, located on the old Leonine walls. Both are probably by Ferrabosco, who with Maderno and Vasanzio contributed much to the decoration of the gardens.

Within Vatican City there are two Colleges: the **Ethiopian College,** for the training of young clergy of the Ethiopian rite, and the **Teutonic College,** which includes an institute for historical and archaeological studies, a library and a cemetery.

Chapter Two

THE SQUARE AND THE BASILICA OF SAINT PETER

The Square

The pilgrim or tourist who comes to visit Saint Peter's is welcomed—one might say embraced—by the majestic curved colonnade that encloses the immense square in front of the Basilica. It is a masterpiece of architecture by Bernini.

The square is a great ellipse 240 metres wide. At the far side, beyond the broad trapezoidal space between the arms of the colonnade and the atrium of the Basilica, rises the façade by Maderno.

Each of the lateral half-circles is formed by an imposing portico of four rows of Doric columns. This colossal structure required 284 columns and 88 pillars. Ninety-six statues of saints stand atop the work.

The colonnade is 18.6 metres high, and it encloses an ellipse of 148 metres by 198 metres. Bernini, who by order of Alexander VII (1655-1667) carried out this great work between 1656

St Peter's Square, with the Basilica and the Apostolic Palace

and 1667, succeeded in symbolizing the motherhood of the Church, as she gathers all nations together in a loving embrace.

In the centre of the square is a 25.88-metre-high Egyptian Obelisk resting upon the backs of four bronze lions. The Obelisk once adorned Nero's Circus, where Saint Peter was martyred. Inserted in the topmost part of the monument is a relic of the True Cross. By order of Sixtus V (1585-1590) the Obelisk was

erected here by Domenico Fontana in 1586. The points of the
compass are marked out around its base. Two fountains, fourteen
metres high, were constructed on either side of the Obelisk,
the one on the right by Maderno (1613) and the one on the left
by Carlo Fontana (1670). Two round stones, located between
the Obelisk and each of the two fountains, mark the focal points
of the ellipse. Looking at the colonnade from either of these

points, the visitor has the impression that it consists of a single row of columns.

To the left of the square beyond the colonnade is the Audience Hall, built by the architect Pier Luigi Nervi and inaugurated by Paul VI on 30 June 1971. It can seat seven thousand people or provide standing room for twelve thousand. The main entrance is from Piazza del Sant'Uffizio.

Between the Basilica and the Apostolic Palace part of the renowned Sistine Chapel, which contains Michaelangelo's master-pieces of painting, can be seen from Saint Peter's Square. Visitors can reach the Chapel by way of the Vatican Museums.

The Apostolic Palace

The Apostolic Palace rises at the right of Bernini's colonnade.

This complex of buildings grew steadily from the 13th to the 19th centuries. Nicholas III (1277-1280) built the central section and additions were made by the two architects Domenico and Carlo Fontana at the direction of Sixtus V (1585-1590). The main entrance to the Palace is called the **Bronze Door.** Beyond it is the Scala Regia or Royal Staircase, while on the right is the Staircase of Pius IX leading to the Cortile di San Damaso. Over-looking this Courtyard are the three **Loggias of Raphael,** the

The inside of the Audience Hall

second of which was painted by Raphael himself. A description will be given below.

The private apartments of the Pope are on the top floor. At noon on Sundays and holy days the Holy Father comes to the second window from the right overlooking Saint Peter's Square, addresses the people gathered below, prays with them and gives them his blessing.

On the second floor is the papal apartment for audiences; it consists of a series of rooms leading to the Pope's Library. Here official audiences are granted to individuals and small groups.

On Wednesdays the Pope usually receives pilgrims in a general audience. This is held in the Audience Hall in the Vatican, except during the summer, when it takes place at Castelgandolfo.

The Papal Villa at Castelgandolfo:
the Theatre of Domitian

Gardens of the Papal Villa at Castelgandolfo

For a short period in the summer months the Holy Father moves to Castelgandolfo, where he continues his usual work in surroundings that are quieter and healthier.

The brief Sunday meeting with pilgrims then takes place from the balcony of the Villa. The Pope's words are simultaneously heard over loudspeakers in Saint Peter's Square.

The following also form part of the Apostolic Palace complex: the **Pauline Chapel,** built by Paul III (1534-1549), with frescoes by Michelangelo; the **Borgia Apartment,** once that of Alexander VI (1492-1503), with frescoes for the most part by Pinturicchio; above these, the **Rooms of Raphael** and the **Chapel of Nicholas V,** with frescoes by Fra Angelico. Access to these famous works of art is through the Museums.

The Basilica

Saint Peter's Basilica, built over the tomb of the Apostle chosen by Christ to be the visible head of his Church, has the strongest appeal for everyone who comes to Rome whether for religious or cultural reasons.

Saint Peter's is above all a place of worship and prayer and it therefore demands the greatest reverence on the part of every visitor. In it are held inspiring liturgical ceremonies often presided over by the Pope. On these occasions a **Papal Choir** performs the musical accompaniment of the rites. It was founded in the distant past and is commonly called the *Sistine Choir,* after Sixtus IV (1471-1484), who re-established it and encouraged its development.

1. The Martyrdom of St Peter and the Memorial of the Apostle

In the Vatican Basilica, beneath Michelangelo's dome, is the papal altar, surmounted by Gian Lorenzo Bernini's bronze baldacchino.

The papal altar is situated exactly above the Tomb of St Peter. The centuries-old tradition of the Church states that Peter, the Fisherman from Galilee, came to Rome, the capital of the Empire, to preach the Gospel, that under Nero he suffered martyrdom in the Vatican Circus, dying like Christ on the Cross, and that later the Emperor Constantine built above his tomb the first church in his honour. All these statements are confirmed by reliable sources, and in particular by the researches promoted by Pius XII and his successors between 1940 and 1964.

From the elements at our disposal, it can now be stated that

Mosaic copy in St Peter's of Guido Reni's Crucifixion of St Peter
The original painting is in the Vatican Picture Gallery

Peter suffered martyrdom shortly after the famous fire of Rome in July, 64 AD, and probably in the autumn of that year. His martyrdom took place in Nero's Circus in the Vatican. His body was taken down from the cross and buried, certainly by pious Christians, beyond the road that skirted the Circus, in a part of the *Ager Vaticanus* already used as a burial ground. The original tomb was a simple grave dug out of the earth, but from the beginning it seems to have been the object of special care.

After Nero's death in June 68 the Vatican Circus soon fell into disuse. However, there still remained to mark the spot the obelisk that in 1586 was removed by Sixtus V and transported to the centre of St Peter's Square. In the second and third centuries the Circus became a necropolis properly speaking. The owners of the new and elaborate mausoleums were pagan families, some of which were gradually being converted to the new faith. But the progressive extension of building activity did not encroach on the area of Peter's tomb, to which the Christians continued to accord ever increasing veneration.

Shortly after the middle of the second century, there was constructed above the ancient grave of St Peter a small funerary building, similar to others dating from the Rome of this period. The building consisted of two niches, placed one above the other, divided horizontally by a slab of travertine supported by two miniature marble columns. The niches were set into a wall, which modern scholars have called the Red Wall, from the bright red colour of the plaster surface. The Red Wall, constructed at the same time as the building, served two purposes: it marked off the area of St Peter's tomb from the burial ground situated behind it (to the west), and at the same time provided a dignified background for the building. In the pavement of the building there was an opening, giving access to the ancient grave containing St Peter's remains. In front of the building, on the eastern side, there was a small open space measuring about seven by four metres, which is now called by archaeologists " Area P ". This was the space left clear out of respect, in front of St Peter's tomb. Scholars now agree in identifying this building as the *trophy* (meaning *glorious tomb*) of St Peter in the Vatican, which was mentioned by Gaius, a learned Roman ecclesiastic, towards the end of the second century.

In the course of the third century, this holy place underwent a certain amount of modification. Immediately to the right of the building and at right angles to the Red Wall there was built another wall, known by scholars as " Wall G ". Whatever its original purpose may have been, it is a fact that between the end of the third century and the beginning of the fourth its north-facing surface came to be covered by a large number of Christian graffiti—rough inscriptions scratched on the wall. These were written in Latin, and were deciphered between 1953 and 1957. It has been possible to distinguish the names of Christ, Mary and Peter, the last-mentioned often indicated by the letters PE, and sometimes joined together in the shape of a Key: ℗. The names are surrounded by numerous invocations and formulas of greeting recommending the names of many dead people. A formula celebrating the victory of Christ, Peter and Mary also appears several times.

The early decades of the fourth century were decisive in the history of the Church, and they also saw notable alterations to Peter's Memorial. After the peace with the Church (313), the Emperor Constantine decided to adorn Rome with Christian basilicas, one of which was dedicated to St Peter. In order to build it, it was necessary to bury completely a considerable section of the large necropolis that stretched from west to east, in front of the Apostle's tomb. This work began shortly after 320, but even earlier—perhaps about 315—the Emperor had the Memorial fittingly arranged. Thus there was constructed the Constantinian monument in honour of St Peter, which partly survives to this day. It consists of a rectangular prism, in which are enclosed the second century building (the *trophy* mentioned by Gaius) the section of the Red Wall containing it, and Wall G with its graffiti. On three sides, to the north, west and south,

*Wall G showing the graffiti, with the loculus
of the Constantinian monument below*

the monument was adorned with slabs of precious Phrygian
marble and royal porphyry, but on the eastern side (the side
facing the entrance to the Basilica) it left visible the front of
the second century building with its lower niche and its table
of travertine supported by the two small marble columns. The

whole was enclosed with a high bronze railing and adorned with six spiralling columns of precious marble decorated with sprigs of vine. Constantine had had these columns brought to Rome from Greece, and later Gian Lorenzo Bernini was to take from them the inspiration for his famous bronze baldacchino.

The people of Constantine's time considered the monument to be the actual tomb of St Peter. Inside, it contains a space specially hollowed out in the thickness of the wall and lined with strips of marble. Inside this space was found a pile of bones, encrusted with earth, together with the remains of a rich cloth. Careful scientific investigations (archaeological, petrographical, chemical and anthropological), carried out between 1962 and 1964, have shown that the space was hollowed out of the wall in the time of Constantine and that from that time onwards it had been always closed and inaccessible from the outside. They further showed that the bones are encrusted with earth of the same type as that in Peter's grave, that the fabric remains come from an ancient cloth of purple embroidered with gold, and finally that the bones are those of a single individual whose characteristics could well correspond to those of the Apostle. Using the data provided by science, one may therefore believe that these bones are the remains of the First of the Apostles. They must have been removed from the ground in Constantine's time, probably as a precaution against the marked dampness of the spot (in fact the original earth grave was found when excavated to be collapsed and empty), and then placed inside the space specially hollowed out of the wall that was being built at this time. Thus they would seem to have come down to us, after nearly twenty centuries.

In the course of time three altars were built over Constantine's monument: first, that of Gregory the Great (590-604), then that of Calixtus II (1119-1124), which enclosed that of Gregory, and finally that of Clement VIII (1592-1605), which is the papal altar of the present Basilica.

At the foot of the papal altar is the open space of the Confession, which is a sort of unroofed chapel surrounded by a high balustrade. On the rear wall of the chapel, behind an artistic railing, is the so-called Niche of the Palliums, in which the *Palliums* (sacred vestments reserved to the Pope and certain bishops) are kept in a precious casket. This spot is the lower niche of the second century building, that is, the *trophy* of Gaius. It stands above the site of the ancient tomb, and beside it is the " loculus " of the Wall *G* that later received the remains mentioned above. If one looks at the Niche of the Palliums, the loculus of Wall *G* is on the right, where the wall is noticeably wider than on the left-hand side. This assymetry may be explained by the need to keep intact Wall *G,* the site of the second tomb.

This therefore is the first foundation on which the papal altar rests, and, at the same time, is the first origin of the Vatican Basilica.

2. The Constantinian Basilica

The Constantinian Basilica was consecrated on 18 November 326 by Pope Sylvester, but was completed only in 349. It was a magnificent building with a nave and four aisles. Before it stood a large colonnaded atrium in the centre of which was a fountain for ablutions. There were many mosaics, frescoes and monuments, some of which are now to be seen in the Vatican Grottoes, where the mortal remains of some of the Popes and some of the Emperors of the West are buried.

Nicholas V (1447-1455) decided to restore the Basilica, and entrusted the work of rebuilding to Bernardo Rossellino in 1452. It seems that the Pope was inspired by Leon Battista Alberti, who, apart from drawing up a building plan for the development of the city, had prepared a plan for the fundamental restoration of the Basilica. There were serious grounds for concern because the Constantinian building was showing signs of decay and

Prospectiua ante gradus
Scalarū ueteris Vaticane
Basilice

Palatiú Archipresbyteri a Leone III.

opus musiuū Pauli primi

Menianū ad bene:
diciones ab Alexan:
dro VI.

Frons Palatij
Paulo 2ᵉ

Grimaldi's design for the façade of St Peter's

disintegration. The southern wall was jutting out almost two
metres; inside, the paintings in the nave and aisles were so
faded as to be scarcely distinguishable. But the Pope died three
years later and the work remained practically at a standstill for
almost half a century.

In the Constantinian Basilica great artists such as Giotto,
Gaddi and Cavallini had exercised their skill, but their works
have been lost, either because of the events that troubled Rome
for a great part of the Middle Ages, or because of the restorations
under Nicholas V, or—and above all—because of the demolition

begun during the pontificate of Julius II (1503-1513). Nevertheless, some sculptures were saved and are now to be found in the Vatican Grottoes. They constitute a little-known chapter of the art of the 15th century. The Constantinian Basilica certainly was a source of inspiration to pilgrims for its sacred character and its wealth of decoration, with its pavement of huge slabs of coloured marble, its stained glass windows, hanging lamps of gold and silver, bas-reliefs and statues, oriental draperies and Flemish tapestries.

3. **Construction of the present Basilica**

Donato Bramante's plans for the new Basilica are known only in broad outline through a drawing by Antonio Sangallo. They were based upon the classical ideal of a simple centrally-planned space with a hemispherical dome over the main area and a smaller cupola over each of its four equal arms. On 17 April 1506 Julius II laid the first stone of the new church in the left pillar that was to support the dome. Demolition of the old Basilica, starting with the transept, began immediately. On the death of Bramante (11 April 1514) a board of three architects was set up, consisting of Sangallo, Raphael and Fra Giocondo da Verona. These men draw up a new plan, with the result that Bramante's Greek-cross concept was radically modified by a considerable lengthening of the nave.

In 1520 both Raphael and Fra Giocondo died, and Baldassarre Peruzzi was appointed to work with Sangallo. These two undid a great part of what had already been accomplished. The Sack of Rome in 1527 and its tragic consequences further slowed down the pace of the work. With the death of Peruzzi in 1536, Antonio Sangallo assumed sole direction, and at the end of 1539 he began laying the foundations of the apse in line with a plan that radically modified the plans of Bramante and Peruzzi. In 1538 a dividing wall was put up between the eleventh and twelfth columns of the nave, in order to make possible the celebration of the liturgy by the canons and visits by the faithful while the work progressed. This wall was demolished in April 1615, when the lengthening of the nave decided on by Paul V was also completed.

The level of the Constantinian Basilica was raised by about three metres. It is not known for certain why this was done. In the resulting space are the Old and New *Grottoes.*

About 1546 Michelangelo reluctantly assumed direction of the work, and asked for and obtained from Paul III (1534-1549) a free hand over everything and everyone. Returning to Bramante's idea of a central ground-plan, he undid Sangallo's work, beginning with the immense outer walls. He made every effort to hasten the work so that no further modifications would be possible.

Between 1551 and 1557 Michelangelo worked hard at bringing his plan to realization. He finished the right transept completely and erected on the four central pillars the base of the dome and the drum with its coupled columns. In November 1558 he began to build a wooden model of the dome and completed it in 1561.

At the death of Michelangelo, Pius IV (1559-1565) appointed Giacomo Barozzi, known as Vignola, Architect of the Fabbrica and ordered him to follow Michelangelo's plan faithfully. Under Saint Pius V (1566-1572) there was no advance in the work. However, in spite of being engrossed by the war against the Turks, this Pope spent large sums for the study of the techniques to be employed in constructing the dome. The studies were taken up again with vigour under Gregory XIII (1572-1585), who entrusted them to Vignola, who came from the same part of

Italy as the Pope and for some time now had been Architect of the Fabbrica. The results, however, were negligible. Della Porta too, who was appointed Architect in 1572, was reluctant to undertake the immense problem of completing the dome. It was only at the energetic urging of Sixtus V (1585-1590) and with the decisive aid of Domenico Fontana that 15 July 1588 saw the beginning of the construction of the huge dome. The Pope hastened the work and completed it in twenty-two months with the placing on 14 May 1590 of the last stone, inscribed with his name, on the topmost point.

Paul V (1605-1622) returned to the Latin-cross plan. This was for liturgical reasons and for the purpose of covering the space formerly occupied by the first Basilica. In September 1605 he gave orders for the demolition of the remaining half of the Constantinian edifice. Carlo Maderno then lengthened the eastern arm of the Basilica, transforming it into a nave and two aisles and extending it as far as the present façade. On 22 November 1614 (although the date given on the frieze is 1612) the walls of the " new Saint Peter's " could be considered completed and those of the old totally demolished. On 18 November 1626 Urban VIII (1625-1644) consecrated the new church.

The present Basilica of Saint Peter's has an area of 15.160 square metres and an internal length of 186 metres. The total length, including the atrium and the thickness of the walls, is 211.5 metres. It is interesting to compare this last figure with the length of some others of the world's biggest churches: Saint Paul's in London (158 metres), the Cathedral of Milan (157 metres), the Cathedral of Florence (149 metres), San Petronio in Bologna (132 metres), Hagia Sophia in Istanbul (110 metres).

The atrium is 71 metres wide, 13.50 metres deep and 20 metres

Interior of St Peter's

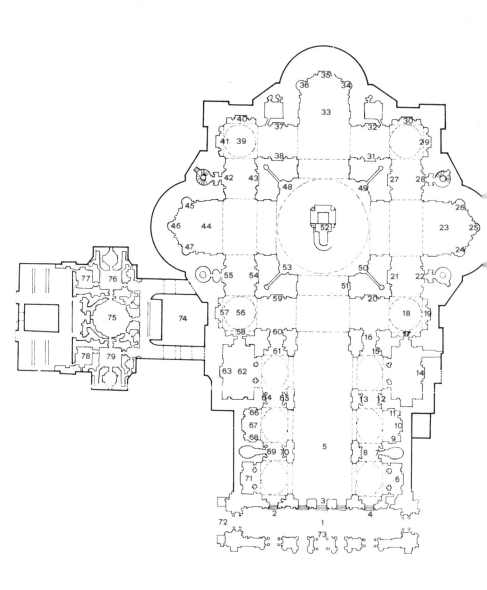

Plan of St Peter's Basilica

1 Atrium
2 Door of the Dead
3 Central Door (by Filarete)
4 Holy Door
5 Nave
6 Chapel of the Pietà
7 Monument to Leo XII
8 Monument to Christina of Sweden
9 Monument to Pius XI
10 Chapel of St Sebastian
11 Monument to Pius XII
12 Monument to Innocent XII
13 Monument to the Countess Mathilde
14 Chapel of the Blessed Sacrament
15 Monument to Gregory XIII
16 Monument to Gregory XIV
17 Monument to Gregory XVI
18 Gregorian Chapel
19 Altar of Our Lady of Perpetual Help
20 Altar of St Jerome
21 Altar of St Basil
22 Monument to Benedict XIV
23 Right transept
24 Altar of St Wenceslas
25 Altar of SS Processus and Martinian
26 Altar of St Erasmus
27 Altar of the Incense-boat
28 Monument to Clement XIII
29 Altar of the Archangel Michael
30 Altar of St. Petronilla
31 Altar of St Peter and the Raising of Tabitha
32 Monument to Clement X
33 Nave of the Chair
34 Monument to Urban VIII
35 St Peter's Chair
36 Monument to Paul III
37 Monument to Alexander VIII
38 Altar of St Peter and the Healing of the Cripple
39 Chapel of the Column
40 Altar of St Leo the Great

41 Altar of the Column
42 Monument to Alexander VII
43 Altar of the Sacred Heart
44 Left transept
45 Altar of St Thomas
46 Altar of St Joseph
47 Altar of the Crucifixion of St Peter
48 Statue of St Veronica
49 Statue of St Helena
50 Statue of St Longinus
51 Statue of St Peter
52 Confession and Papal Altar
53 Statue of St Andrew (entrance to Grottoes)
54 Altar of the Candlestick
55 Monument to Pius VIII (door to Sacristy)
56 Clementine Chapel
57 Altar of St Gregory
58 Monument to Pius VII
59 Altar of the Transfiguration
60 Monument to Leo XI
61 Monument to Innocent XI
62 Choir Chapel
63 Altar of the Immaculate Conception
64 Monument to St Pius X
65 Monument to Innocent VIII
66 Monument to John XXIII
67 Chapel of the Presentation of the Virgin
68 Monument to Benedict XV
69 Monument to Maria Clementina Sobiesky (entrance to Dome)
70 Stuart Monument
71 Baptistery
72 Arch of the Bells
73 Mosaic of the " Navicella "
74 Largo Braschi
75 Sacristy
76 Sacristy of the Beneficiaries
77 Historical Museum
78 Chapter Room
79 Sacristy of the Canons

high. The façade is 114.69 metres wide and 45.44 metres high. The nave is 44 metres high and 27.50 wide. The diameter of the dome is 42 metres, which is 1.40 metres less than the dome of the Pantheon. But while the height of the latter is only 43.40 metres, that of the dome of Saint Peter's to the top of the cross is 132.50 metres.

The church is furnished with 44 altars and 395 statues: 104 of marble, 161 of travertine, 40 of bronze and 90 of stucco.

4. The main works of art of the Basilica

The broad façade of Saint Peter's Basilica, built by Carlo Maderno between 1607 and 1614, is reached by a wide triple flight of steps. At the foot of this stairway, on either side, are two colossal statues of Saint Peter and Saint Paul. The former is by Giuseppe De Fabris and the latter by Adamo Tadolini; they were placed here about the year 1840.

A single row of huge Corinthian columns and pilasters extends across the entire façade, in the centre of which is the " Loggia " of Blessings, from which the Pope imparts the *Urbi et Orbi* blessing. From the same Loggia, a few minutes after the end of the conclave which elects a new Pope, the senior cardinal deacon proclaims to the crowd the name of the one who has been elected, with the words: *Annuntio vobis gaudium magnum: habemus papam ...* (I announce to you a great joy, we have a Pope ...), and the new Pontiff imparts to the world his first Apostolic Blessing.

The Basilica is entered through five doors. The one on the extreme right is the *Holy Door,* which is opened and closed personally by the Pope at the beginning and end of jubilee years. During the Jubilee proclaimed by the Pope—a practice which

St Peter's Basilica: Bernini's bronze baldacchino over the papal altar

was begun in 1300 and at first was held every hundred years, then every fifty and now twenty-five years—the faithful can gain special indulgences.

As one enters the Basilica one is vividly impressed by the majestic nave. Before reaching the Confession, one sees at the far end on the right the venerated bronze statue of Saint Peter seated and giving his blessing. The right foot has been worn smooth by the kisses of pilgrims. The statue was formerly believed to be a work of the 5th century, but it may be by the 13th century sculptor Arnolfo di Cambio.

Beyond the statue one finds oneself beneath the dome, which surmounts four great arches resting upon enormous pillars.

In the centre, above the papal altar, stands the famous bronze Baldacchino by Bernini. It was begun before 1624 and inaugurated by Urban VIII on the vigil of the Feast of SS. Peter and Paul in 1633. The altar, built by Maderno, is called the Altar of the Confession, because it is located immediately above the tomb of the Apostle who by his martyrdom confessed his faith in Christ. Ninety-five lamps are kept continually burning on the encircling balustrade and cast their light upon the tomb of the Fisherman from Galilee. In front of the tomb is a statue of Pius VI in prayer, by Canova.

In the first chapel of the right-hand aisle is Michelangelo's most important and famous work, the *Pietà*. Michelangelo completed it in 1500 when he was barely twenty-five years old. The dead body of Christ taken from the cross lies in Our Lady's lap. This is the only work that bears Michelangelo's signature, which is plainly visible on the band crossing the Virgin's breast. An unbalanced person damaged the statue in May of 1972; within the same year it was restored.

The next chapel has the shape of an ellipse. It contains a crucifix attributed to Cavallini (thirteenth century). Opposite is the monument of Queen Christina of Sweden. Next is a large chapel containing Francesco Messina's statue of Pius XII, which was unveiled by Paul VI. On the other side of the chapel is a statue of Pius XI by Francesco Nagni.

St Peter's Basilica: Michelangelo's Pietà

*St Peter's Basilica: The Chair by Bernini
in the apse of the nave*

Also worthy of note in the right hand aisle is the *Chapel of the Blessed Sacrament,* enclosed by an iron grille designed by Borromini. The chapel is famous for its precious Tabernacle of gilded bronze, flanked by two angels kneeling in adoration. It was executed by Bernini in 1674. Here the Blessed Sacrament is reserved, and Holy Communion is given to the faithful at Mass and at other times during the day.

At the end of the aisle is a mosaic copy of The *Communion of Saint Jerome* by Domenichino; the original is in the Vatican Picture Gallery.

Also at the end of this aisle one finds on the right the area known as the *Gregorian Chapel.* It was built in the time of Gregory XIII by Giacomo Della Porta (1585). The corresponding area opening off the end of the left aisle is called the *Clementine Chapel.* It too is by Giacomo Della Porta.

Returning along the left aisle towards the entrance, one comes to the *Choir Chapel,* designed by Carlo Maderno. Beyond it is the monument to Saint Pius X (1903-1914) by the architect Florestano Di Fausto and the sculptor Enrico Astorri (1923). The Pope is represented in the act of invoking peace at the time of the 1914-1918 war. His mortal remains are kept in a crystal casket in the nearby Chapel of the Presentation. Opposite his monument is the celebrated bronze monument of Innocent VIII by Antonio Pollaiolo, the most ancient one in the Basilica.

The large *Chapel of the Presentation* beyond these two monuments contains on the right a bas-relief in honour of John XXIII by Emilio Greco, while on the left is the monument of Benedict XV by Pietro Canonica.

Continuing on towards the entrance, one comes to the Baptismal Font, made of an ancient sarcophagus of red porphyry. The Chapel in which it stands was designed by Carlo Fontana and contains some of the best mosaic pictures in the Basilica: The Baptism of Christ by Maratta, SS. Processus and Martinian by Passeri, and Cornelius the Centurion by Procaccini.

The nave and aisles lead to the transepts. The one on the right is named after SS. *Processus and Martinian,* its central altar being dedicated to these martyrs. In this spacious area, close to the Gregorian Chapel, were held the sessions of the First Vatican Council in 1870.

One of Canova's most famous works, the monument of Clement XIII, stands in the passage from the right transept to the *Chapel of Saint Michael.* This Chapel takes its name from its mosaic copy of Guido Reni's painting of the archangel.

At the far end of the Basilica there stands out distinctly the majestic baroque *Cathedra* or Chair, executed by Bernini during the pontificate of Alexander VII (1655-1667). It is of bronze with gold highlights. In it was enclosed a wooden chair that from the thirteenth century onwards was believed to be the one used by Saint Peter when preaching. According to the authoritative judgment of certain specialists who at the direction of Paul VI studied the history of the " Chair of Saint Peter ", this precious relic is probably a royal throne of Charles the Bald, given to the Pope of the time about the year 875. Inserted into the front of this throne, which became the papal chair, are panels of precious ivory showing the Labours of Hercules and other figures.

The *bronze Chair* is supported by statues of two doctors of the Latin Church, Saint Ambrose and Saint Augustine, and of two doctors of the Greek Church, Saint Athanasius and Saint John Chrysostom. Above, a radiant sunburst in gilded stucco adorned with angels and clouds encircles a dove, the symbol of the Holy Spirit, who is the soul of the Church. The effect, one of the most beautiful to be found in late baroque, expresses a profound religious idea: the chair is the symbol of the teaching authority of the Church, which has its highest expression in the doctrinal pronouncements of the Pope; the Holy Spirit inspires and guarantees this teaching, according to the promise of Christ, while theological reflection, symbolized by the holy doctors, depends on it and at the same time makes it more widely known and more profoundly understood.

Continuing leftwards, one reaches the *Chapel of Our Lady of the Column.* It contains a relief by Algardi, showing Saint Leo I confronting Attila. From here one passes to the left transept. Its central altar is dedicated to Saint Joseph. The ceiling decorations are by Vanvitelli and Maini.

5. The Grottoes

The Vatican Grottoes are situated in the three-metre-high space between the floor of the present Basilica and that of the ancient Constantinian Basilica. Their construction was begun under Gregory XIII and completed in the time of Clement VIII (1592). Referred to as the *Old Grottoes,* they consist of a crypt in the form of a nave with aisles, with cross-vaulting; they also include six large alcoves, with barrel vaults, situated beneath the Gregorian and Clementine Chapels. The *New Grottoes,* constructed at the order of Clement VIII, continue in the direction of the great dome, below the crossing, and form a semicircle around the *Chapel of Saint Peter* (the Confession), which, as has been noted, is built above the tomb of the Apostle.

From the beginning the sepulchral monuments, frescoes, mosaics, altars and sarcophagi that are all that remains of the old church were transferred here. The most famous of the sarcophagi is that of Junius Bassus, a masterpiece of early Christian sculpture.

Between the years 1940 and 1950 Pius XII had major excavations carried out with a view to improving the lay-out. Ten new rooms were added, to house the ancient works of art that had been kept in the former Museo Petriano or that were actually discovered during the work of excavation.

In the course of this operation the foundations of the Constantinian Basilica were uncovered, and, as has been mentioned, a first-century graveyard was found. Finally, new altars were built and the tombs of seventeen popes, including Pius XII and John XXIII, were arranged in the grottoes.

Important from an artistic and historical point of view are a number of sepulchral mosaics in the *Alcove of the Fisherman;* they are among the oldest ones with a Christian theme. Especially interesting also is the bronze monument of Sixtus IV, considered the masterpiece of Antonio del Pollaiolo (1493).

The Grottoes can be regarded as a link between the demolished Constantinian Basilica and the present one.

6. The Treasury of Saint Peter's

The Sacristy and the Treasury or Artistic and Historical Museum are reached through a door situated between the left transept and the Clementine Chapel, beneath the imposing monument to Pius VIII. In the *rooms of the Treasury* are kept religious furnishings of great value. The collection goes back to the time of Constantine, who, it seems, made the first gifts. But the greater part of the items on view are later than the 18th century, since many precious objects were dispersed in the numerous sackings which Rome underwent in the course of the centuries, but especially when the city was occupied by Napoleon. By the Treaty of Tolentino in 1796 the Holy See was compelled to hand over to the French army the sum of ten million tornesi, and precious objects to the value of a further five million. Gold and silver were melted down and priceless masterpieces of silverware surrendered.

7. Access to the Dome

The entrance for going up to the Dome is also located in the left hand aisle, beneath the monument to Maria Clementina Sobieski. The first part of the ascent—as far as the terrace above the central nave—can be made by lift or on foot. From the terrace can be seen Michelangelo's majestic Dome, rising above ten smaller ones: two are quite large and crown the Gregorian and Clementine chapels; the others, of smaller size, are arranged in two rows above the chapels of the side aisles.

From the terrace it is possible to reach the top of the Dome itself by a staircase built into the space between its inner and outer shells. Thus one reaches the *Panoramic Loggia* surrounding the *lantern;* from here there is an exceptional view of Vatican City State and the City of Rome.

Chapter Three

CHRISTIAN ROME

As Saint Peter's successor, the Pope is also Bishop of Rome. In caring for the diocese he is assisted by a Cardinal Vicar.

The present organization of the **Vicariate of Rome** goes back to 1912.

The Vicariate offices are in the Lateran Palace, which is situated beside the ancient Cathedral of Rome, the Basilica of the Most Holy Saviour, also known as St John Lateran.

The Cardinal Vicar is assisted by either one or two vicegerent archbishops and a number of auxiliary bishops.

Rome is a city very rich in churches. The visitor's interest is concentrated on the more ancient ones, both because of their great store of religious and historical memories and because they are in general more important for the artistic nobility of their architecture and decoration.

Apart from the Basilica of St Peter, three churches enjoy the title of Major or Patriarchal Basilica: St John Lateran, St Mary

Major (both in the city) and St Paul Outside-the-Walls. The last is, like St Peter's, a basilica built over a cemetery outside the city. St Laurence Outside-the-Walls (situated in the square of the same name, at the Campo Verano, the main cemetery of Rome) has from ancient times also been considered a major basilica. In addition, the churches of San Lorenzo in Damaso (in the Palazzo della Cancelleria) and Santa Maria in Trastevere (in the square of the same name in the centre of the Trastevere district) began to be called minor basilicas in mediaeval times. Several other churches also acquired the title of minor basilica, either from popular usage or as a privilege granted by the Pope.

Among the many sacred buildings of special historic and artistic importance one may mention Santa Sabina on the Aventine, San Clemente (in Via S. Giovanni in Laterano, between the Colosseum and the Lateran Basilica), Santa Maria sopra Minerva (in Piazza della Minerva, near the Pantheon, which was a pagan temple later transformed into a Christian church and which contains tombs of famous people, including Raphael), Santa Maria in Cosmedin (in Piazza Bocca della Verità), the Gesù and Sant'Ignazio (in squares of the same names), San Pietro in Montorio (on the Janiculum), Sant'Andrea della Valle and the Chiesa Nuova (in Corso Vittorio Emanuele), Sant'Agnese in Agone (in Piazza Navona), San Gregorio and SS John and Paul on the Caelian Hill (near the Colosseum), the nearby Church of Santa Maria in Domnica alla Navicella, St Peter-in-Chains (which houses the statue of Moses by Michelangelo, also near the Colosseum), Sant'Agnese fuori le Mura (a Constantinian basilica, on Via Nomentana), Santa Maria in Aracoeli (on the Campidoglio) and Santa Cecilia in Trastevere (in the square of the same name).

Particularly evocative are the places and monuments of ancient Rome connected with the first establishment of the Christian faith. Among these are the various Catacombs (which will be considered later) and the Mamertine Prison, which adjoins the Church of San Giuseppe de' Falegnami in the Roman Forum (Via Clivo Argentario). It was an ancient Roman public prison and, according to tradition, among those imprisoned in it was Saint Peter, under the Emperor Nero.

Basilica of St John Lateran

Tradition says that it was founded by Pope Melchiades (311-314) on a piece of land given by the Emperor Constantine. A confirmation of this is to be found in the fact that Constantine's second wife, Fausta, was a sister of Maxentius, and recent excavations have shown that the Basilica was built over the barracks of the *equites singulares,* who formed part of the forces of Maxentius. The original church, which had a nave and double aisles, was dedicated to Christ the Saviour and only later to St John the Baptist, the Precursor of Christ, and to St John the Evangelist, Apostle and author of the Fourth Gospel. The Constantinian Basilica was sacked by the Vandals in 455 and was restored by St Leo the Great (440-461) and later by Adrian I (722-795). It was severely damaged by an earthquake in 896 and rebuilt by Sergius III in 905. Nicholas IV (1288-1292) enriched it with lavish decorations. Twice destroyed by fire, in 1308 and 1361, it was largely restored by Urban V (1362-1370) and Gregory XI (1371-1378), with Giovanni di Stefano from Siena as architect.

The main façade was restored by Clement XII (1730-1740) and is one of the finest architectural works in Rome. Leo XIII (1878-1903) had the apse restored, and the work was completed in 1885.

In the Basilica and the adjoining Palace were held the Ecume-

Basilica of St John Lateran:
main façade

nical Councils of 1123, 1139, 1179, 1215 and 1512; for this reason they are called the Lateran Councils.

The **main façade,** the work of Alessandro Galilei, is decorated with a majestic loggia of arches. On top of the cornice are fourteen statues of apostle and saints, dominated by the large figure of the Saviour with the Cross. The interior has a nave and double aisles. The imposing ceiling is decorated with the arms of the Popes.

On each of the **twelve pillars** of the nave is a shrine designed by Borromini and containing a massive statue of one of the Apostles. Above these are artistic high reliefs, designed by Alessandro Albardi in 1659 and depicting scenes from the Old and New Testaments.

The **transept** was completely renovated in the pontificate of Clement VIII (1597-1601). This work was entrusted to Giacomo Della Porta and Il Cavaliere d'Arpino.

In the centre of the transept is the papal altar, which was restored in 1851. In the upper part is preserved a wooden altar which an old tradition asserts was used by St Peter and his successors. At the foot of the altar is the tombstone of Martin V (1417-1431), a highly artistic work by Simone Ghini.

The **sanctuary** and **apse** are dominated by a wonderful mosaic executed by Jacopo Torriti and Jacopo da Camerino between 1288 and 1294. The upper part depicts the Saviour among the clouds and surrounded by angels; in the middle is the heavenly Jerusalem from which flow four rivers (representing the Gospels) to slake the thirst of the sheep and deer shown below.

Also of major interest are the following: a fresco, possibly by Giotto and of great historical significance, representing Boniface VIII proclaiming the Jubilee of 1300 (first pillar of the right-hand intermediary aisle); the monument of Cardinal Martinez, the work of Isaia da Pisa, and the cosmatesque tomb of Cardinal Casati (both in the outer aisle on the right). An architectural masterpiece is the Corsini Chapel, the work of Galilei, in which is to be seen a fine *Pietà* by Antonio Montauti.

Near the rear of the Basilica, in Piazza San Giovanni in Laterano, is the Baptistry. It was built by Constantine, but practi-

Interior of St John Lateran's, showing papal altar,
Gothic tabernacle and the apse

cally rebuilt about the year 440 by Sixtus III and given its present appearance in 1637 by Urban VIII.

Towards the centre of the piazza rises an Egyptian obelisk of red granite. It dates from the fifteenth century B.C. and was brought from Thebes in Egypt by Constantius II in a ship specially built for the purpose. It is the tallest and oldest obelisk in Rome: it stands 47 metres high including the base. It was Sixtus V who transferred it from its original site in the Circus Maximus, where it lay badly damaged, restored it and in 1588 erected it in front of the Lateran Basilica.

Adjacent to the Basilica of St John Lateran, on the right-hand side as one looks towards the main façade, is preserved the **Scala Santa,** so called from an undocumented tradition which holds that it is the staircase of the Praetorium of Pilate in Jerusalem which Jesus ascended and descended several times on the day of his trial and condemnation to death. It consists of 28 steps, which the faithful ascend on their knees out of devotion. According to the tradition just mentioned it was brought to Rome in 325 by St Helena, mother of the Emperor Constantine.

Basilica of St Mary Major

From Saint John Lateran the Via Merulana leads to the Basilica of Saint Mary Major, the second of the Patriarchal Basilicas within the city. It is also called the Liberian Basilica after Pope Liberius (352-366). According to an ancient tradition, this Pope traced out the perimeter of the Church after the *miraculous snowfall* which is said to have occurred during the night of

5 August in an unstated year of his pontificate. The building was entirely reconstructed in the fifth century by Sixtus III (432-440), who in memory of the Council of Ephesus, at which the Divine Motherhood of the Blessed Virgin was proclaimed, had the famous mosaics of the triumphal arch executed. It was the first church in Rome to be dedicated to the Mother of the Saviour.

Gregory XI (1370-1378) had the campanile built. It is the highest one in Rome. Sixtus V and Paul V added the two side chapels, which consequently are known as the Sixtine and Pauline chapels.

The **main façade** of the Basilica was designed and constructed by Fuga (1741-1749) during the pontificate of Benedict XIV (1740-1758). In the upper portico is the wonderful thirteenth-century mosaic by Filippo Rusuti, a pupil of Cavallini.

The **loggia** is built on to the old façade of the Basilica, and preserves the latter's decoration, consisting of two series of mosaics. The upper series depicts Christ in the act of blessing, Our Lady with a number of saints, angels and symbols of the Evangelists; the lower series shows Pope Liberius and several historical events connected with his construction of the old Basilica.

The interior of the Basilica is eighty-six metres long. It is extremely spacious and harmonious, divided according to classical proportions into a nave and aisles, in a perfect reproduction of the model of the early Christian basilicas. Nave and aisles are divided by monolithic columns with Ionic capitals. The ceiling, which is attributed to Giuliano da Sangallo, is composed of 105 coffers divided into five rows. Tradition states that the gilding was carried out with the first gold brought from the New World.

Basilica of St Mary Major

On the left as one enters is the monument to Nicholas IV (1288-1292) by Domenico Fontana and Leonardo da Sarzana. On the other side is the monument of Clement IX (1667-1669) by Carlo Rainaldi and Domenico Guidi.

In the Sixtine Chapel, which has already been mentioned, is a tabernacle by Torrigiani, made according to a design by Domenico Fontana. Near the front of the altar is the *Oratory of the Crib,* with the relic held by tradition to be the crib of Bethlehem. Along the walls of the Chapel are two monuments, also designed

Interior of St Mary Major's:
mosaic by Torriti in the apse

by Fontana, which commemorate Sixtus V (1585-1590) and St Pius V (1566-1572).

The Pauline or Borghese Chapel was built by the architect Flaminio Ponzio. It contains the tombs of Clement VIII (1592-1605) and Paul V (1605-1621). The paintings in the chapel are by several artists, including Guido Reni, but the most important one is that of Cur Lady *Salus Populi Romani*. This ancient icon is thought to be of the ninth century, and the veneration in which it is held by the people of Rome is shown by great signs of piety and devotion. Of particular interest in the right-hand aisle is the modest tomb of Giánlorenzo Bernini. It was commissioned by his son Lorenzo, who was a canon of the Basilica.

Cn the walls of the nave are to be seen twenty-seven mosaic pictures of the time of Sixtus III (432-440), precious examples which show that the best art of the late Roman Empire was already being used in the fifth century to celebrate the mysteries of the Christian faith. There are twelve on the left-hand wall and fifteen on the other. Those on the right depict Moses and Joshua, while those on the left show scenes from the lives of Abraham, Isaac and Jacob. At the front of the nave other mosaics depict the Annunciation, and episodes from the infancy of Christ, such as the Epiphany, the Massacre of the Innocents, the Presentation of Jesus in the Temple and the Flight into Egypt. In the vault of the apse the Triumph of Mary is depicted in the great mosaic of Jacopo Torriti, which shows her being crowned by the enthroned Christ. At the sides of the throne are eighteen angels. The work was carried out at the command of Nicholas IV (1288-1292), who himself appears in the lower part of the mosaic.

In the apse there are also four bas-reliefs by Mino del Reame (fifteenth century) representing, on the right, the Assumption of Our Lady and the Epiphany, and on the left the Crib and the miracle of the snow.

In the right-hand aisle is the Baptistry by Flaminio Ponzio (1605). The font consists of a large porphyry basin and was made by Valadier in 1825. Next to the font is a fine relief by Pietro Bernini depicting the Assumption of the Blessed Virgin.

In the square in front of the Basilica rises a tall marble column, the only one remaining of the eight which once adorned the Basilica of Maxentius. It was placed on this spot in 1614 by Maderno. At the top there is a bronze representation of the Mother and Child, by Guillaume Berthelot. At the foot of the column is a fountain, a reminder as it were to the People of God to drink from the Source of grace, whose mother is Mary.

Basilica of St Paul Outside-the-Walls

This is the largest of the Major Basilicas after St Peter's. It was originally built by Constantine over the tomb of St Paul, the persecutor of Christians who was transformed by Christ into the Apostle of the Nations and who was beheaded in Rome about the year 67.

Enlarged by Valentinian II in 386 and later by the Emperor Theodosius I, the old Basilica consisted of a broad nave and four aisles divided by eighty columns. At that time it was the largest church in the Christian world, a distinction it retained until the building of the present Basilica of St Peter.

The Basilica was almost completely destroyed by fire in 1823. It was rebuilt by the architects Bosio, Camporesi, Belli and Poletti during the pontificates of Leo XII (1823-1829) and Pius IX (1846-1878). The latter Pope consecrated the new building in 1854.

The fire occurred a few days before the death of Pius VII, and the sad news was kept from him.

The mortal remains of St Paul the Apostle, who together with St Peter founded the Church of Rome, lie in the casket under the high altar. The stone covering the tomb bears the simple inscription *Paulo apostolo mart.* It was discovered in 1834 during the rebuilding operations and according to some authorities it dates from the fourth century, but others doubt its authenticity.

Entering the square portico, designed by Poletti and carried out by Vespignani and Calderini, one sees in the centre the statue of St Paul by Canonica. On the façade are mosaics carried out according to designs by Consonni and Agricola. They represent the four Major Prophets, Isaiah, Jeremiah, Ezechiel and Daniel. At the top is the figure of Christ between SS Peter and Paul.

The modern damascened bronze door is by Antonio Maraini.

Basilica of St Paul's Outside-the-Walls

It has ten panels which illustrate the lives of the Apostles Peter and Paul. Inside on the right has been placed, at the wish of Pope Paul VI, a magnificent bronze door, recently restored, which was made in Constantinople for Gregory VII (1073-1085) by Staurachios of Chios. It is one of the finest examples of Byzantine art and consists of fifty-four panels representing figures of prophets and scenes from the life of Christ, with Greek inscriptions. The door is likewise one of the most noteworthy examples of mediaeval silversmiths' work.

On entering the Basilica one cannot fail to be struck by the clear architectural arrangement, which is enhanced by the coffered ceiling and by the thirty-six frescoes that Pius IX had painted on the walls. Of particular interest are the portraits of the entire series of Popes which line the walls of the nave, even though modern scholarship is not agreed about the accuracy of the succession indicated here.

Nave of St Paul's Outside-the-Walls

At the far end a majestic apse completes the Basilica. The light filters through alabaster windows and gives the building an atmosphere of religious recollection.

The central nave ends with the statues of SS Peter and Paul, the work of Fabris and Tadolini respectively.

In the apse, a mosaic which has been restored several times develops the theme of Christ as Judge. Standing beside him are SS Peter, Andrew, Luke and Paul. At his feet is Pope Honorius II (1216-1227), who had the work carried out by three Venetian masters.

A little lower down is the Triumph of the Passion, with the Cross on an altar between angels, apostles and the Holy Innocents.

The Basilica has seven altars: the papal altar, two in the transepts and four in the side chapels.

There is a noteworthy cloister, which is attributed to Vasseletti and his son, who also made the large paschal candlestick which stands in the transept. In the cloister are preserved fragments of the fabric of the old Basilica, together with a large Roman sarcophagus known as that of Pietro di Leone, who was buried in it in the year 1100. It bears representations of episodes connected with the god Apollo.

There is a museum on the upper floor of the monastery of the Benedictine monks who have charge of the Basilica. The museum contains collection of ancient Christian inscriptions and tombstones from the Constantinian Basilica and a series of forty-two frescoed medallions of Popes, beginning with St Peter. These medallions decorated the old Basilica before it was burnt down.

The Catacombs

The numerous Roman catacombs are entrusted to the Holy See by virtue of article 33 of the Concordat with Italy. The Holy See provides for their preservation, supervision, maintenance and scientific exploration.

The catacombs are among the most venerated shrines of the Christian world and their history can be divided into different periods.

From their origin around the middle of the second century A.D. until the beginning of the fifth century, they were the cemeteries of the *titles* or parishes of the Christian community in Rome.

In the first half of the fifth century burial in underground galleries came to an end and the catacombs became exclusively places of pilgrimage. Near them churches were built or already existing ones enlarged. Areas in the vicinity were set aside where pilgrims could rest. The crypts were decorated, lit with lanterns and linked by direct staircases to the surface. The catacombs that did not possess tombs of martyrs disappeared from memory. For the sake of pilgrims guidebooks were written, some of which, dating from the seventh and eighth centuries, have survived to this day and are the most valuable and reliable sources for archaeologists.

Towards the end of the eighth century pilgrimages by Christians to the tombs of the martyrs began to diminish and finally stopped altogether. The suburbs of Rome, which had been sacked several times by the Lombards, were now in a state of abandonment, and in the midst of the general poverty the Popes were unable to restore and maintain properly all the churches of the martyrs. As a consequence of this, and since in other regions, especially the East, there had already begun the practice of transferring the bodies of martyrs to churches and oratories, the Popes decided to bring the remains inside the walls of the city. This marked the end of the catacombs. The churches above ground slowly crumbled, and the entrances to the galleries disappeared under the rubble. Within a few years the existence of most of the original catacombs had been forgotten. Only a few galleries near San Sebastiano, on the Via Appia, part of the famous ceme-

Cubiculum in the Catacomb of Domitilla, showing the deceased being led into heaven by the martyr Petronilla

tery *ad catacumbas,* continued to be visited throughout the entire Middle Ages.

It cannot be said with certainty when each of the cemeteries was rediscovered in the modern era, though much credit for this work is given to Antonio Bosio (1575-1629) who is called the *Columbus of the world beneath the surface of Rome.* Bosio uncovered approximately thirty catacombs and laid the foundations for later scientific research through his topographical analysis of the monuments in the light of available documents. The archaeologists of the seventeenth and eighteenth centuries however did not follow Bosio's topographical method. They began to despoil the catacombs by transferring inscriptions and sarcophagi to museums and churches. They opened a large number of tombs in search of presumed bodies of martyrs, which they thought to recognize through the presence of little vessels containing reddish stains. The countryfolk of the surrounding areas completed the work of destruction by removing material for building their farms. Large areas of the cemeteries were thus left in a state of devastation and neglect.

In the last century, with the establishment by Pius IX of the Pontifical Commission for Sacred Archaeology, this situation came to an end. Gian Battista De Rossi (1822-1894) took up the work of scientific research and traced the dominant lines for Christian archaeology. His excavations brought to light many shrines of martyrs which, hidden under the rubble, had fortunately escaped the ravages of previous centuries. He demonstrated how the glorious pages of the history of the first Christian centuries could be read in the fragments of the monuments. His studies stimulated fresh research, which subsequently extended to other parts of the ancient world. The Roman catacombs remained the model for these studies.

Within approximately three kilometres of the Aurelian Walls more than forty catacombs have been discovered. They are to be found along the principal consular roads, since Roman law forbade burial within the city. Every catacomb has its own history. Some were established on private property through the kind permission of the owner. In other cases, when the Christian community of Rome became more organized and began to have possessions in common, individual parishes undertook the establishment of a site for burying their dead. The catacombs excavated on private sites generally retain the name of the owner: Balbina, Calixtus, Domitilla, Maximus, Pontianus, Praetextatus, Priscilla, Thraso, etc. The desire to make the maximum use of the available space led the Christians of Rome, where the subsoil is of soft yet resistant rock, to imitate the Etruscan burial-vaults: the dead were placed one above the other in rectangular niches hewn out of the walls of underground tunnels. These niches are called *loculi*. The passageways are about one metre wide and generally between two and three metres high. From a principal passage other secondary galleries branch out, usually at right angles; thus there is created a network containing thousands of tombs.

In the *loculi*, generally made to measure, the dead were placed wrapped in a shroud and sometimes coated with lime as a cheap form of embalming. Even two or three bodies may be found in one tomb. The loculus was closed with tiles or a slab of marble cemented in with lime. On the slab or tiles the name of the deceased was painted or chiselled, or simply scratched into the lime. For the purpose of recognition the relatives often placed in the wall a single coin, or an ivory figure, or a piece of ceramic. They also often enclosed a small vase containing perfume or a small oil lamp.

A richer form of burial is the *arcosolium*, with the sealing slab placed horizontally and, above it, an arch, very often plastered and decorated with frescoes. This type of tomb was especially used in the *cubicula*, small rooms that every so often open out from the walls of the passages and which are family tombs. Here are to be found most of the frescoes which are the great attraction of the catacombs. More rarely there are sarcophagi, rectangular caskets of carved marble.

In these paintings and carvings, as well as in the inscriptions, sentiments of invocation, of good wishes and of prayer are

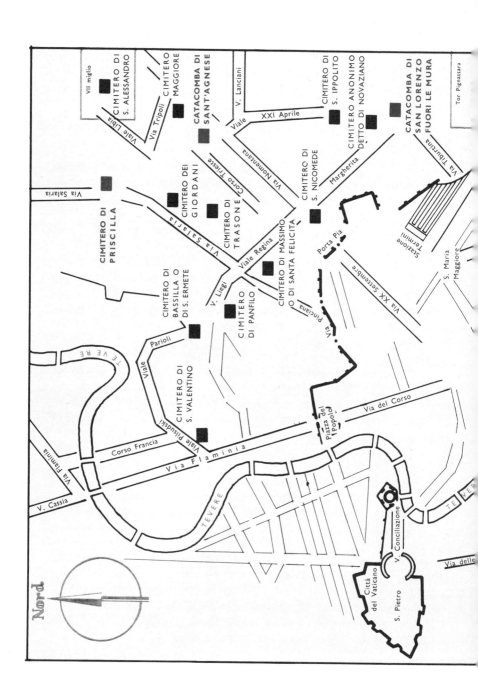

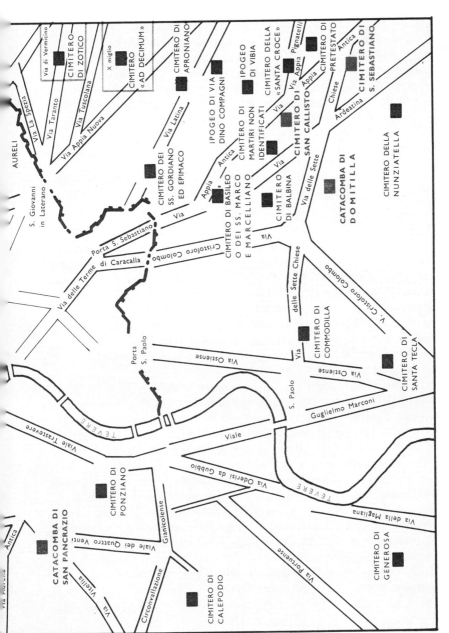

Plan of the Roman catacombs.
Parts open to the public shown in red

expressed. The word " cemeteries ", which was applied by Christians to their burial places, means " dormitories ", that is, temporary places of rest in expectation of a new life. The catacombs thus enable us to relive the history of the first Christian generations, who expressed in their cemeteries the faith that sustained them in persecution and trial, their confidence in God's help and their certainty of resurrection. The deceased in fact are always represented in an attitude of prayer or as already in possession of eternal happiness.

The following pages treat of the principal ancient Christian cemeteries that are normally open to the public.

The **Catacomb of Saint Sebastian** on the Via Appia Antica. It would be more exact to call this the *Memorial of the Apostles,* the name given it in ancient documents, in view of the unmistakable signs of a cult of the Apostles Peter and Paul dating from the middle of the third century. There is a banquet room or *triclia* with the walls covered with invocations to the founders of the Church of Rome written by visitors. Many sarcophagi in the museum bear a representation of the two Apostles. In their honour a great basilica was built over the triclia in the Constantinian period; it was of a special shape and was surrounded by tombs.

Three earlier pagan tombs have been found under the triclia. These were covered over when the latter was built. They contain elegant stuccoes and paintings showing funeral ceremonies. There is also a very important Christian inscription: the Greek letters *IXTΘYC*, the initial letters of the phrase *Iesús Christós Theoú Yiós Sotér* (Jesus Christ Son of God Saviour) with a " T ", symbolizing the Cross, inserted. These letters form the Greek word meaning " fish ", and a fish is engraved on the marble of various humble tombs in the surrounding catacombs, which date from the second century. There are two Roman villas with frescoes of the second and third centuries. In the fourth century the catacomb was extended in the vicinity of the crypt of Sebastian, martyred during the Diocletian persecution. The remains of another martyr, Saint Quirinus, were brought here from distant Pannonia in the fifth century by Christians fleeing before the

*The Good Shepherd, on the vault of a cubiculum
in the Catacomb of St Calixtus*

invading barbarians, and buried in a great tomb behind the apse
of the basilica. This tomb was called the " Platonia ".

The **Catacomb of Saint Calixtus** is also on the Via Appia Antica.
It is the oldest official cemetery of the Christian community of
Rome. The popes of the third century were buried here. Nine
of them are in the Crypt of the Popes: Saint Pontianus (230-235),
Saint Anterus (235-236), Saint Fabian (236-250), Saint Lucius I
(253-254), Saint Stephen I (254-257), Saint Sixtus II (257-258),

Saint Dionysius (259-268), Saint Felix I (269-274), and Saint Euty-chianus (275-283). In the nearby crypts are buried Saint Gaius (283-296), Saint Eusebius (309 or 310), Saint Miltiades (311-314), and Saint Cornelius (251-253). Various inscriptions on the tombs give the names followed by the qualification *episcopus* (bishop) and in some instances *martyr*. De Rossi also discovered fragments of three poems composed in their honour by Pope Saint Dama-sus I, who was devoted to the cult of the martyrs. The fragments are inscribed in fine *philocalian* lettering.

Another crypt was the burial place of Saint Cecilia, who is represented in a ninth-century fresco preserved here. Other famous martyrs buried in this cemetery were Tarcisius, the martyr of the Eucharist, Calogerus and Parthenius. There are many paintings, of which the second-century ones in the crypt of Lucina are very important, as are also those in the Crypts of the

Christ among the Twelve Apostles:
arcosolium in the Catacomb of Domitilla

Sacraments (so called because of their symbolism referring to baptism and the Eucharist). The cemetery is very extensive and at some points there are as many as five galleries one above the other. Some of the " cubicula " are built in a grandiose style with wide openings in the ceiling to admit light.

The **Catacomb of Domitilla** on the Via Ardeatina contains equally large tombs and is bigger in area than that of Saint Calixtus. It takes its name from the martyr Flavia Domitilla. She was a relative of the emperor Domitian and a daughter of the sister of the consul Flavius Clemens, another martyr who died in the persecution that broke out at the end of the first century (Eusebius, *H. E.* III:18:4). The Christian Flavii had donated the land for the cemetery. It has been discovered that this cemetery originally consisted of four separate nuclei, which were later joined together by the network of galleries. One of these nuclei is called the Hypogeum of the Flavii, although it is not really connected with that family. It contains a wide gallery for sarcophagi, a room for funeral meals and a well.

The most striking thing about this catacomb is the unexpected great aisled basilica. It is lit from above and thus one can appreciate the depth at which it is buried. It is dedicated to Saint Nereus and Saint Achilleus, two soldier martyrs, who were honoured by Pope Damasus with a fine epigram which is displayed at the entrance. The altar was placed over their tomb and all the surrounding galleries were demolished to make room for the basilica, which was built between 390 and 395. In a crypt behind the apse is a fresco representing another martyr of the catacombs, Saint Petronilla, shown leading a deceased woman into paradise. The cemetery is rich in paintings and important epigraphs.

The **Catacomb of Priscilla** on the Via Salaria Nuova is one of the most ancient and extensive in Rome. It gets its name from its owner, who is mentioned in an epitaph in which she is given the title of *clarissima,* indicating that she was a member of the nobility. The catacomb was greatly extended during the third and fourth centuries. Here were buried the martyrs Felix and

Philip, Crescention, Prisca, Potentiana, Praxedes, Phimes and others whose names are unknown, as well as Popes Marcellinus (296-308), Marcellus I (308-309), Sylvester I (314-335), Liberius (352-366), Siricius (384-399), Celestine I (422-432), and Vigilius (537-555). The network of underground corridors is on two levels, of which the upper is the more ancient. It contains paintings and stuccoes of the earliest period of Christian art, with scenes from the Old and New Testaments. Worthy of note is the fresco of the *Breaking of Bread,* which has reference to the miracle of the multiplication of the loaves and to the Eucharistic banquet. There are two paintings of the Virgin Mary dating from the first half of the third century, the most ancient that exist. In one she is shown with the Child in her arms and a prophet beside her; in the other she is seen seated, with an angel in front of her, a clear reference to the Annunciation. When the rear walls of the main gallery were demolished a number of very ancient graves were discovered, most of them belonging to the ordinary faithful. In another part is an important " cubiculum " of the end of the third century, with scenes showing the prophet Jonah, the sacrifice of Abraham, the three young men in the fiery furnace, and the Good Shepherd. Covering the whole of the back wall there is a large fresco which may represent the consecration *(velatio)* of a virgin.

There are other catacombs open to the public near the following basilicas: **Saint Laurence Outside-the-Walls** (Via Ciriaca) the burial-place of the deacon Laurence, the Church's standard-bearer during the persecution of Valerian; **Saint Pancras** (Porta San Pancrazio), with the tomb of the saintly youth who is the patron of the newly-baptized but whose identity is not historically verifiable; **Saint Agnes** (Via Nomentana), the cemetery in which was buried the twelve-year-old girl whose martyrdom deeply moved her contemporaries and the ecclesiastical writers of the 4th century.

The city has other notable Christian catacombs which are not normally open to the public. We shall give the reader a brief description only.

At the beginning of the Via Aurelia Antica is situated, apart from the already-mentioned cemetery of Saint Pancras, the *cemetery of Calepodius* (Via di Vigna Armellini), the most ancient Christian catacomb in the Trastevere district. It contains the tomb of Pope Saint Calixtus, who died in 222. This is the oldest tomb of a Pope so far discovered, after that of Saint Peter.

In the vicinity of the Via Portuense, which in ancient times led to the port of Rome (near the modern Fiumicino), are the *cemetery of Pontianus* (Via Alessandro Poerio), which contains what was probably a baptistry, with a fresco of the Baptism of Christ, and the *cemetery of Generosa* (Via della Magliana), which has an important fourth-century fresco showing the Saviour surrounded by martyrs.

Along the Via Ostiense, apart from the tomb of Saint Paul in the Major Basilica named after him, is to be found the *cemetery of Commodilla* (Via delle Sette Chiese), with an unusual small underground basilica and with two fourth-century pictures, one of Christ among saints and another of Our Lady, also surrounded by saints. Also on the Via Ostiense is the *cemetery of Saint Thecla* (Via Laurentina), which is notable for the fine architecture of the cubicula, which have floors at a level below that of the galleries, an arrangement not found elsewhere.

Along the Via Ardeatina, besides the catacomb of Domitilla, is the *cemetery of Basileus,* also called that of *SS Mark and*

Catacomb of Pamphilus: gallery with intact loculi

Marcellianus, which is lavishly decorated with scenes from the
Bible. Here too is the *cemetery of Balbina* (or of Pope Mark, 336).
It is not certain whether this is a separate cemetery or part of
the nearby unnamed *cemetery of unidentified martyrs*, which has
yet to be explored.

The area richest in Christian burial remains is that running
along the Via Appia Antica, the *Queen of Roads*, which is also
lined by fine memorials of the leading families of Ancient Rome.
Apart from the large catacombs of Saint Calixtus and Saint Se-

bastian, along this road are situated the *Hypogeum of Vibia,* an interesting example of a mixed cemetery, that is, one containing both Christian and pagan tombs, the *cemetery " of the Holy Cross ",* so-called because it contains a painting of a typical equilateral cross, and the *cemetery of Praetextatus* (Via Appia Pignatelli), which resulted from the meeting of several originally separate burial grounds. The last-named contains many well preserved frescoes.

Around the Via Latina are grouped the *cemetery of SS Gordian and Epimachus,* the *cemetery of Apronianus* (Via Cesare Correnti), the important *Hypogeum of Via Dino Compagni,* consisting of thirteen " cubicula " and niches, the walls of which are covered with frescoes and remind one of a modern picture-gallery, and finally the *cemetery " ad decimum ",* that is, at the tenth milestone along the road.

Near the ancient Via Labicana are: the *Hypogeum of the Aurelii* (Via Luigi Luzzati), with large frescoes differing completely from the usual Christian style of decoration; the *cemetery of Saints Marcellinus and Peter* (Via Torpignattara), where the Four Crowned Martyrs were buried (Clement, Sempronianus, Claudius and Nicostratus); the *cemetery of Zoticus* (Via di Vermicino), a small country catacomb at the bottom of the hill on which Frascati stands.

In the area of the Via Tiburtina, apart from the cemetery of Cyriaca or Saint Laurence, is the so-called *cemetery of Novatianus* (Viale Regina Margherita), in which four finely decorated sarcophagi were found, and the *cemetery of Saint Hippolytus,* which is interesting mainly for a number of inscriptions relating to various places of worship in the city.

Apart from the cemetery of Saint Agnes, the Via Nomentana has the *cemetery of Saint Nicomedes* (Via Villini), the *Greater cemetery* (Via Asmara)—so called to distinguish it from the *Lesser* one nearby, discovered recently—which contains a number of " thrones " carved out of the rock, and the *cemetery of Saint Alexander* (at the seventh milestone along the Via Nomentana), the burial-place of Christians from the present Mentana and other settlements near the city.

The Via Salaria Nuova and the Via Salaria Vecchia also have several ancient Christian cemeteries, the most important being the Catacomb of Saint Priscilla, which has already been described. Mention may also be made of the *cemetery of Maximus* or *Saint Felicity* (Via Simeto), which contains some interesting inscriptions; the *cemeteries of the Jordani and Thraso* (Via Taro and Via Yser); an *unnamed cemetery* (Via Anapo) containing a typical picture of Christ among the twelve Apostles; the *cemetery of Pamphilus* (Via Giovanni Paisiello), with galleries which are the deepest of all the Roman catacombs and contain many still intact " loculi "; the *cemetery of Bassilla* or Saint *Hermes* (Via Bertoloni), which incorporates a spacious underground basilica.

At the beginning of the ancient Via Flaminia, in the modern Viale Parioli, is the *cemetery of Saint Valentine*, which also has an important and fairly well preserved basilica.

National Churches and Pontifical Institutes of Learning

As the centre of the Catholic world, Rome offers pilgrims and visitors from all lands churches where they can gather for prayer, celebrate the Eucharist and find priests from their own country or speaking their own language who can provide spiritual assistance. The need for such facilites has always been felt, as is shown by the fact that many of the national churches were built centuries ago and in several cases are of great architectural and artistic interest.

The following list may be of interest to the visitor:

Croatian language: San Girolamo (Via di Ripetta, 181).

English language: Saint Clement's (Via San Giovanni in Laterano, 45-47).

Saint Isidore's (Via degli Artisti, 41).

Our Lady of the Blessed Sacrament and the Canadian Martyrs (Via G. B. Rossi, 46).

Saint Patrick's (Via Boncompagni, 31).

San Silvestro in Capite (Piazza San Silvestro).

Santa Susanna (Via Venti Settembre, 15).

Saint Thomas of Canterbury (Via di Monserrato, 45).

French language: Santi Claudio e Andrea dei Borgognoni (Piazza San Claudio al Tritone).

San Giuliano dei Belgi (Via del Sudario, 40).

San Luigi dei Francesi a Campo Marzio (Piazza San Luigi dei Francesi, 5).

German language: Santa Maria dell'Anima (Via della Pace, 20).

Polish language: Santo Stanislao (Via delle Botteghe Oscure, 15).

Portuguese language: Sant'Antonio in Campo Marzio (Via dei Portoghesi, 2).

Spanish language: Santa Maria di Monserrato (Via Giulia, 151).

Nostra Signora di Guadalupe e San Filippo Neri (Via Aurelia, 675).

Santi Quaranta Martiri e San Pasquale Baylon (Via San Francesco a Ripa, 20).

In Rome there are also several churches of the Eastern Rites. The main ones are:

Armenian Rite: San Nicola da Tolentino (Via San Nicola da Tolentino, 17).

Romanian Byzantine Rite: San Salvatore alle Coppelle (Piazza delle Coppelle, 72-B).

Russian Byzantine Rite: Sant'Antonio Abate all'Esquilino (Via Carlo Alberto, 2).

Greek Byzantine Rite: Sant'Atanasio al Babuino (Via dei Greci, 36).

Greek Melchite Rite: Santa Maria in Cosmedin (Piazza Bocca della Verità).

Syro-Antiochian Rite: Santa Maria in Campo Marzio (Piazza Campo Marzio, 45).

Syro-Maronite Rite: San Marone (Via Aurora, 8).

97

In the city of Rome are several Pontifical Institutes for theological and ecclesiastical studies: They are:

The *Pontifical Gregorian University* and the related *Pontifical Biblical Institute* and *Pontifical Oriental Institute*. These are run by the Society of Jesus (Jesuits) and are situated in Piazza della Pilotta, except for the Oriental Institute, which is in Piazza Santa Maria Maggiore, 7.

The *Pontifical Lateran University*, entrusted to the care of the clergy of Rome and situated at Piazza San Giovanni in Laterano, 4.

The *Pontifical Urban University*, which is able to confer degrees also in the missiological sciences. It is situated at Via Urbano VIII, 16.

The *Pontifical University of Saint Thomas Aquinas*, run by the Order of Preachers (Dominicans) and situated at Largo Angelicum, 1.

The *Pontifical Institute of Saint Anselm*, run by the Benedictine Fathers and situated at Piazza dei Cavalieri di Malta, 5.

The *Pontifical Institute of Saint Anthony (Antonianum)*, directed by the Order of Friars Minor and situated at Via Merulana, 124.

The *Pontifical Salesian Institute*, with the *Pontifical Higher Institute of Latin Studies*, run by the Salesian Fathers and situated in Piazza dell'Ateneo Salesiano, 1.

In addition to these institutes, the following should be noted: the Pontifical Theological Faculties of *Saint Bonaventure* (Via del Serafico, 1), of *Saints Teresa of Jesus* and *John of the Cross* (Piazza San Pancrazio, 5) and the *Marianum* (Viale 30 Aprile, 6); the Pontifical Institutes of *Sacred Music* (Piazza Sant'Agostino, 20), of *Christian Archaeology* (Via Napoleone III, 1), of *Arabic Studies* (Piazza Sant'Apollinare, 49); and finally the *Pontifical Institute " Regina Mundi "*, for the theological training of women religious (Lungotevere Tor di Nona, 7).

Chapter Four

THE
VATICAN
MUSEUMS

The papal museums and galleries, as art collections open to the public, were initiated at the wish of Clement XIV (1769-1774) and Pius VI (1775-1799). Hence they were first called the " Pio-Clementine Museum ". Pius VII (1800-1823) expanded them considerably, adding the Chiaramonti Museum, the New Wing and the Gallery of Inscriptions.

Gregory XVI (1831-1846) founded the Etruscan Museum (1837) for the antiquities excavated in southern Etruria from 1828 onwards; the Egyptian Museum (1839) for housing objects brought from explorations in Egypt and other Egyptian works previously kept in various galleries of classical art, including the Capitoline Museum; and the Pagan Museum of the Lateran (1843) for statues, bas-reliefs and mosaics of the Roman period that could not be housed in the Vatican Palace.

In 1854 Pius IX (1846-1878) added to the Pagan Museum the Christian Museum of the Lateran, which contained ancient Christian sculptures, especially sarcophagi and inscriptions. Later (1856-1869) he also added two rooms to house objects taken from the excavations carried out at Ostia during those years. At the direction of John XXIII (1958-1963) these two collections were transferred from the Lateran Palace to a specially erected new building in the Vatican. In 1970 the collections were again opened to the public, under the name of the Gregorian Pagan Museum and the Pian Christian Museum.

The Museums also include: the Tapestry Gallery, containing a collection of tapestries of various kinds dating from the sixteenth century; the Gallery of Maps, begun by Gregory XIII (1572-1585) and completed by Urban VIII (1623-1644); the Hall of Modern Paintings; the Hall of the Immaculate Conception; the Rooms and Loggia of Raphael, decorated for Julius II (1503-1513) and Leo X (1513-1521); the Chapel of Fra Angelico, painted during the pontificate of Nicholas V (1447-1455); the Sistine Chapel, so called from its founder Sixtus IV (1471-1484); the Borgia Apartment, where Alexander VI (1492-1503) once lived and which was restored and opened to the public by Leo XIII (1878-1903) in 1897; the Vatican Picture Gallery, formerly situated in the apartment of Gregory XIII on the third loggia, transferred by Saint Pius X (1903-1914) in 1909 to the wing of the Library facing the Gardens, and in 1932 placed by Pius XI (1922-1939) in a special building near the new entrance to the Museums; the Missionary and Ethnological Museum, founded by Pius XI in 1926 and arranged on the upper floors of the Lateran Palace, and transferred with the others mentioned above to the Vatican at the wish of John XXIII; and the Profane and the Sacred Museums of the Apostolic Vatican Library.

These museums, galleries and other halls can be reached from the entrance to the Vatican Museums on Viale Vaticano.

The Gregorian Egyptian Museum

The first collection of Egyptian antiquities in the Vatican was made by Pius VII (1800-1823), who bought them on the advice of Canova. To this first collection were added papyri and objects brought to Rome by Franciscan missionaries. Pius VII himself directed that this valuable material should have a museum set aside for it in the rooms below the Etruscan Museum, and entrusted its arrangement and decoration to the Egyptologists Father Ungarelli and de Fabris. The work was speeded up and completed in the pontificate of Gregory XVI (1831-1846), and it was due to this latter pope, whose aims were connected with apologetics rather than culture alone, that the Egyptian Museum was opened on 2 February 1839, the first such museum in history. As Ungarelli wrote, the material collected here shows evidence of traditions preceding the written revelation of the period beginning with Moses, as well as of traditions shared by the people of the Ancient Covenant and the Egyptians. In the museum were also placed a number of Egyptian works that had been in Rome since the time of the emperors or at Hadrian's Villa near Tivoli.

The Museum occupies ten rooms. The **first,** the **Room of the Sarcophagi,** contains *sarcophagi* in black basalt dating from the sixth century B. C. together with *statues* of animal-headed anthropomorphic deities.

Next comes the **Room of the Statues.** Here is to be seen the *Head of Pharaoh Mentuhotep IV* (2054-2008 B. C.), the oldest pharaonic portrait in the Museum. There are also two colossal black granite statues, bearing inscriptions, of the *goddess Sekhmet,* daughter of the Sun, dating from the thirteenth century B. C.

Queen Tuaa

Special mention should be made of the *throne of a seated statue of Rameses II* (1292-1225 B.C.), who is said to have persecuted the Hebrews and in whose reign tradition holds that Moses was born. The finest statue however is considered to be that of *Queen Tuaa*, which is of dark granite and dates from 1280 B.C.

The **third room** is known as the **Room of the Imitations,** since it contains Egyptian-style sculptures and bas-reliefs by second and third-century A.D. Roman artists. These works come from the Tivoli area. The best known are the statue of the *Personified Nile* and a *bust of the goddess Isis.*

The **fourth room** is the **Room of the Naophorus,** taking its name from a basalt statuette of *Psammeteksenb* portrayed as a *naophorus* (i.e. " carrying a temple "). Psammeteksenb was a physician and dentist of the XXVIth Dynasty (sixth century B. C.). The Room also contains another *naophorus* statue of an unknown person and a fine *statuette of the naophorus Udjeharresnet.* Along the left wall is a display cabinet containing the *Vatican Papyrus of the Book of the Dead,* recently restored and preserved in inert gas.

The **fifth room** is that of the **Hemicycle.** Here are to be seen a number of cabinets containing restored *mummy-cases.* Worthy of note is the statue of The *Beautiful Woman,* near the entrance, and further on the throne of a lost sculpture of Pharaoh Rameses II. In the centre of the hemicycle is a colossal statue of the *mother* of Rameses II.

Five small rooms follow, containing *mummies, scarabs, statues* of other *naophori* of various periods, as well as *papyri* of different centuries, almost all of a funerary character. The papyri contain formulas and prayers and are of outstanding scientific value for the variants occurring in their hieroglyphic and hieratic scripts.

The Pio-Clementine Museum

The Pio-Clementine Museum was founded in the last decades of the eighteenth century in order to provide a worthy setting for the important works of sculpture that had been brought together in the Vatican from the sixteenth century onwards.

Clement XIV (1770-1774) decided to arrange the collection as a " Papal Museum ", and the building was planned and erected by the architects Dori, Simonetti and Camporese.

The new building linked the west wing of the library to what had been the summer residence of Innocent VIII. Later, Pius VI (1775-1799) ordered the construction of an extension to the building, which was consequently named the *Pio-Clementine Museum.*

This forms the first section of the Vatican sculpture museums, and the entrance opens on to what is known as the *Vestibule of the Four Gates,* adjacent to the Picture Gallery Courtyard. It consists of a number of halls in which are arranged 1,445 priceless sculptures.

The Hall of the Greek Cross: a harmonious neo-classical room designed by Michelangelo Simonetti (1780). In the place of honour at the entrance is a bust of Pius VI.

At the sides are two *reclining sphinxes* in reddish-grey granite dating from the Roman period. Of particular importance is the great porphyry *sarcophagus of Constantia* (or Constantina), daughter of the emperor Constantine the Great (fourth century). Opposite is the *sarcophagus of Saint Helena,* Constantine's mother. Some hold that this sarcophagus was intended for Constantine himself and they adduce as confirmation the high-reliefs of battle scenes with Romans on horseback and chained or fallen barbarians. In the centre of the hall is a mosaic depicting a shield bearing a *bust of Minerva and the phases of the moon* (third century). Two red granite *telamones* (statues in the Egyptian style and functioning architecturally as supports) found in Hadrian's Villa near Tivoli frame the entrance to the next hall.

The **Circular Hall:** a masterpiece by Simonetti, inspired by the Pantheon. Ancient *mosaics* adorn the floor. In the centre is

The Round Hall in the Pio-Clementine Museum

a huge *porphyry vase,* thirteen metres in circumference, which appears to have been found in the *Domus Aurea* of Nero. Eight niches contain colossal *statues of divinities* and deified heroes; among them is a bust of *Trajan's wife,* a statue of *Juno* (second century A. D.), and a statue of the *emperor Claudius* represented as Jupiter. One of the most important pieces in this hall is the statue of an *enthroned emperor,* believed to be Galba or Nerva, which seems to date from the first century A. D. Also of great interest is a *bust of Antinoüs,* drowned in the Nile in 130 A. D. and deified by the emperor Hadrian, who was present at his death, and a *statue of Hercules* in gilt bronze, of the first century B. C. or the first century A. D., and which is thought to have been struck by lightning. The last-mentioned was brought to the Vatican after its discovery in 1864 during excavations in the area of Pompey's Theatre.

Meleager

The **Hall of the Muses** takes its name from the *statues of the Muses* placed in it. Seven of them were found near Tivoli in 1774, together with the statue of Apollo also to be seen here. They date from about the third century A. D.

The hall is octagonal, with a vestibule at either end and containing sixteen Corinthian columns. The vaulted ceiling is adorned with frescoes by Sebastiano Conca representing Apollo and the Muses.

Special mention should be made of the *herma* (portrait bust on a pillar) of *Pericles* wearing a Corinthian helmet, the symbol of Athenian generals. Of great artistic worth are the *hermae and busts of Antisthenes, Periander* and others. Also notable are the *heads of Epicurus* (d. 270 B. C., founder of Epicureanism), of the *poet Homer* (eighth century B. C.), of *Socrates* (d. 399 B. C.), of *Plato* (d. 347 B. C.) and of *Euripides* (d. 406 B. C.).

In the centre of the hall is a coloured mosaic of the *Head of Medusa.*

The **Hall of the Animals:** The most important work here is considered to be the *statue of Meleager* with his dog and the head of the boar that he has killed. It is a Roman work of the second century A. D., a copy of a Greek original of the fourth century B. C., probably by Scopas.

Original works include the *Crab* in green porphyry, an extremely rare stone, and the group showing *Mithras* slaying the bull. On one wall are two little mosaics made up of minute tesserae; one of them shows bulls being *attacked by a lion.* The black and white mosaic on the floor of the middle section is also interesting; the central panel shows a *falcon devouring a hare;* in the rest of the mosaic are marsh-birds.

The **Gallery** or **Hall of Statues:** Under Clement XIV this was transformed into a sculpture gallery by the architect Dori (d. in 1772). It was extended in 1776 at the direction of Pius VI and linked with the Hall of the Animals; unfortunately this involved the demolition of a chapel frescoed by Mantegna.

The main work to be admired here is the *Apollo Sauroctonos* (" killing a lizard "), a copy of a bronze original by Praxiteles (about 350 B. C.). The god, portrayed as a boy, is leaning gracefully against a tree, watching for the right moment to kill the reptile.

Bust of Julius Caesar

Mention should also be made of the statue of *Hermes*, a Roman work of the second century A. D.; the *Wounded Amazon*, a copy of the bronze original by Phidias (430 B. C.); the *Eros of Centocelle*, the famous copy of a Greek original of the fourth century B. C.; and the *Resting Satyr*, another famous copy of a bronze by Praxiteles.

At the end of the gallery is the *Seated Statue of a Sleeping Woman*, once believed to be Cleopatra. It would seem rather to represent Ariadne abandoned by Theseus. The god Dionysus, by whom she has been chosen, is approaching her as she sleeps.

Bust of Marcus Aurelius

The **Hall of the Busts:** This consists of four small rooms, divided by arches on columns of " giallo antico " and decorated with stucco drapery. Here has been placed the monumental statue of *Jupiter enthroned* and holding the thunderbolt signifying the power of the highest of the gods. This work is a copy of the original gold and ivory statue of the Capitoline Jupiter made by Apollonius in the first century B. C. *Busts of Roman emperors* and other persons are displayed on the walls.

The **Room of the Masks:** The present appearance of this room dates from Pius VI and it takes its name from the four mosaics

The Belvedere Courtyard

of theatrical masks in the pavement. These were found in 1779 in Hadrian's Villa at Tivoli. The ceiling is adorned with oil paintings by Domenico De Angelis of scenes from ancient mythology.

The *Venus of Cnidos* is very famous. It is an important copy of the well-known statue of Aphrodite executed by Praxiteles in the fourth century B. C. The movement of her arm and the slight curving of her body convey the cold sensation felt by the goddess as she enters the water.

Also from Hadrian's Villa at Tivoli is a red *marble Satyr.* Next to it is a group of the *Three Graces,* a second century A. D. Roman copy of a late Hellenistic original.

When the visitor reaches this point he must return to the Hall of the Animals, and there, through a door on his left, on the side opposite the Hall of the Muses, he goes out into the **Belvedere Courtyard.** This was built by Giacomo da Pietrasanta to a design by Bramante, but was later altered by Simonetti (1773), who added the octagonal Ionic portico containing four recesses, or *cabinets,* in which are placed sculptures of exceptional value. A fountain in the middle gives life to the courtyard.

The most important cabinet is that containing the *Laocoön* by the Rhodian sculptors Hagesander, Athanadorus and Polydorus.

The Laocoön group

Recent discoveries in the Cave of Tiberius near Sperlonga have led some authorities to assign these artists to the middle of the second century instead of the first century B. C. The group was found in 1506 in the Esquiline area. Laocoön, a priest of Apollo, and his sons, entwined in the coils of two serpents, stand on the steps of an altar. One snake is about to bite the priest's back; the other has already attacked the younger son, who collapses with pain, while the other son, as yet unharmed, struggles to escape. The punishment of Laocoön is the revenge of the goddess Athena for his having warned the Trojans against the danger of the famous Wooden Horse.

The well-known *Belvedere Apollo,* which was recently freed from unsuitable nineteenth-century restorations, stands in the next *cabinet.* The god is advancing with light step, almost floating. In one hand he holds a bow, the symbol of retribution at a distance, while in the other he carries a sprig of beribboned bay, the sign of the purifying and healing power of the god, who is able also to relieve misfortune. His splendid youthful figure has become a symbol of sublime purity; hence the use of the adjective " Apollonian ". The statue dates from 130 A. D. and is a copy of a Greek original in bronze, attributed to the sculptor Leochares of Athens. It was found at the end of the fifteenth century at Grottaferrata.

Next comes the *Cabinet of Perseus.* This statue is a brilliant creation by Antonio Canova (1800), showing the then fashionable classical influence, of which the Belvedere Apollo is an exemplar.

The Belvedere Apollo (detail)

The Apoxyomenos (detail)

Next, one comes to the statue of *Hermes* or *Mercury*, which gives its name to the fourth oabinet. It was once believed to portray Antinoüs. It is a Roman copy, made in the time of the emperor Hadrian, of a fourth century B.C. Greek original, and was found near Castel Sant'Angelo. The travelling cloak and the lithe movements perfectly represent the messenger of the gods.

Leaving the octagonal courtyard by the door opposite the Hall of the Animals, one enters the **Circular Vestibule,** once part of Innocent VIII's villa. Here is to be seen the *Apoxyomenos* (an athlete scraping the oil from his body), a copy of the bronze original by Lysippus (340-320 B.C.) mentioned by Pliny the Elder in his " Natural History " (34:62). The athlete has returned from the exercise ground and with the strigil in his left hand is scraping the oil, dust and sweat from his outstretched right arm. It is the image not of a winner receiving the usual honours from the crowd but of a tired athlete paying with his fatigue the price of victory. This is a fine example of the realism of the sculptor Lysippus, who represented men not as they appear to be but as they really are.

Also of note is the altar of Augustus (12 B. C.), decorated on all four sides with reliefs.

On the right of the *Circular Vestibule* is the **Vestibule of the Torso.** Here is to be seen the *Belvedere Torso,* which probably represents Hercules. The powerful figure, of which only the torso remains, is seated on the skin of a wild animal. This work was particularly admired by Michelangelo. It is signed by " Apollonius son of Nestor, from Athens " (first century B. C.), an artist of the neo-Attic school, who lived in Rome towards the end of the Republic. The statue was found at the beginning of the fifteenth century.

The Chiaramonti Museum

This museum takes its name from its founder, Pope Pius VII Chiaramonti (1800-1823). It is divided into three parts: the **Chiaramonti Museum** strictly speaking, the **Gallery of Inscriptions,** and the **New Wing.**

The first part was planned by Bramante and partly executed by him. It links the aforementioned Villa of Innocent VIII (also called the Belvedere Palace) with the Papal Palace. Its arrangement is due to Antonio Canova, who worked on it from 1807 to 1810.

View of part of the Chiaramonti Museum

A row of pilasters divides the walls into fifty-nine compartments, thirty on the left and twenty-nine on the right. A thousand or so ancient sculptures of various kinds and qualities are gathered here: Greek originals, copies of statues of divinities, portraits, altars, architectural decorations, urns and sarcophagi. Under Canova's direction, frescoes illustrating Pope Pius VII's activity in favour of art were painted on the fifteen lunettes by artists of St. Luke's Academy.

The **Gallery of Inscriptions** was arranged at about the same time as the Chiaramonti Gallery. The collection which it houses, begun by Clement XIV (1769-1774) and successively enriched down to the time of Pius VII, consists of over five thousand pagan and Christian inscriptions, the former on the left side, the latter (coming largely from the catacombs) on the right.

The **New Wing** was built by Raffaele Stern (1817-1822). It was given this name to distinguish it from the older wing, built for the Library by Fontana at the direction of Sixtus V two hundred and fifty years before. It is a marvellous barrel-vaulted gallery, seventy metres long by eight wide, flanked by niches containing

The Lapidary Gallery

The New Wing of the Chiaramonti Museum

statues of busts on pedestals of precious marble. The pavement is adorned with mosaics from a second-century villa that stood near Tor Marancia on the Via Ardeatina. These depict mythological figures.

The New Wing was brought into use only on the recovery in 1815-1816 of the ancient sculptures taken to Paris by Napoleon by virtue of the Treaty of Tolentino (19 February 1797). The official inauguration took place on 14 February 1822.

Special mention should be made of two works displayed in the Chiaramonti Museum: the *Doryphoros* (spear-bearer) and the Augustus.

The *Doryphoros* is a copy, made at the beginning of the imperial period, of a bronze original attributed to Polyclitus of Sicyon (440 B. C.). Pliny the Elder refers to this type of sculpture when speaking of *effigies Achilleae* (figures of Achilles). The *statue of Augustus* was found in Livia's Villa near Prima Porta on the Via Flaminia. The first Roman Emperor is shown in military dress, with his right arm raised as he makes a speech. His sculptured breastplate commemorates a historical event of 20 B. C.: a Parthian is handing back to an officer of the emperor the standard of the Roman army.

Two other statues are those of the *Nile* and of *Demosthenes*. The river god is identified by the sphinx and crocodile beside him, and is represented as an old man reclining on his cloak and holding a cornucopia of flowers and fruit, the symbol of fertility. Sixteen children, placed on different levels, symbolize the sixteen cubits that the Nile normally rises when it floods the fields and makes them fruitful. On the plinth are reliefs with scenes of life in Egypt or showing hippopotamuses fighting pygmies or crocodiles.

The statue of the orator *Demosthenes* stands in the last niche on the left. Its identification was made possible by comparing it with a bust found in Herculaneum, on the plinth of which his name was inscribed. It probably goes back to a bronze original of 280 B. C. placed in the *Agora* in Athens to commemorate his strenuous efforts to preserve the independence of Greece from Macedonia.

The Apostolic Vatican Library

As mentioned in Chapter I, the idea of setting up the Apostolic Vatican Library was due to Nicholas V (1447-1455).

Later, Sixtus IV (1471-1484) considerably enriched the collection of books and also had the rooms decorated and furnished by Melozzo da Forlì and the Ghirlandaio brothers.

Sixtus V (1585-1590) further increased the Library and commissioned Domenico Fontana to build its splendid present home,

Apostolic Vatican Library: the Sistine Hall

which consists of a long gallery, a spácious hall and other smaller rooms.

Pius XI (1922-1939), who had been prefect of the Ambrosian Library in Milan and who later became prefect of the Vatican Library, equipped the Library with a modern system of shelving.

Included in the Library is the **Clementine Gallery,** divided into five sections at the time of Pius VI (1775-1799) and containing paintings by De Angelis showing *scenes from the life of Pius VII.*

Next comes the **Alexandrine Hall,** which takes its name from Pope Alexander VIII, in whose pontificate it was built in 1690. The frescoes on the walls, also by De Angelis, show *scenes from the life of Pius VI.*

Through the **Pauline Halls,** built by Paul V (1605-1621), the **Sistine Hall** is reached. This was built at the direction of Sixtus V and is elaborately decorated. The architect was Domenico Fontana, who worked on it from 1587 to 1589. The spacious hall is divided by pillars into two aisles. Above the vindows are paintings of monuments of the old Rome of Sixtus V. The pillars are frescoed with allegorical pictures of the inventors of various alphabets.

Two more halls follow, also built at the direction of Sixtus V. They lead to the **Gallery of Urban VIII** (1623-1644). Among the items on display here are some interesting astronomical instruments.

A Roman mosaic preserved in the Pagan Museum of the Library

The Pagan Museum of the Library

This consists of a single hall in which material of various origins is arranged in *cabinets*. Statues, ivories and sculptures of the Etruscan and Roman periods are kept here. The museum was begun under Clement XIII in 1767 and completed by Pius VI (1775-1799). The vault is decorated with a very fine fresco showing *Minerva and Time*.

Mention should be made of the *heads of Augustus and Nero*, both in bronze, and of a second-century Roman mosaic found in Hadrian's Villa near Tivoli.

A reliquary cross, showing New Testament scenes, preserved in the Sacred Museum of the Library

Detail of the Aldobrandini Marriage fresco

The Sacred Museum of the Library

This museum was founded by Benedict XIV in 1756 and contains an interesting selection of examples of the minor Christian arts. It was rearranged by Pius XI (1922-1939).

The **Chapel of Saint Pius V** (1566-1572) contains an altar with a richly embroidered frontal. On the walls are frescoes by Jacopo Zucchi (1541-1589) showing scenes from the *life of Saint Peter of Verona*, a Dominican martyr. In a display cabinet are sacred objects once kept in the chapel of the *Sancta Sanctorum* at the Lateran.

123

In the **next room,** known as the **Vestments Room,** are sacred vestments presented to Clement VIII (1592-1605) by the Grand-Duke of Tuscany.

Particular mention should be made of the rooms in which are kept the most ancient Christian testimonies found in the catacombs, as well as interesting papyri and messages of homage addressed to various popes. The collection of Byzantine ivories and mediaeval enamels in the **third room** is of high artistic value. On the end wall of the same room is displayed a fragment of a mosaic taken from the triclinium of Leo III (795-816) at the Lateran, showing the *head of an apostle.*

In the **Room of the Aldobrandini Marriage** is the famous fresco of that name. It was discovered in the Esquiline area of Rome at the end of 1604, and is one of the finest paintings of the time of Augustus. It is probably a copy of a work of the time of Alexander the Great.

On the walls are paintings of scenes from the *Odyssey,* which were found on the Esquiline in 1848, and the *Famous Women,* pictures found in 1816 at Tor Marancia on the Via Ardeatina, close to the Catacomb of Domitilla.

The pavement is adorned with ancient mosaics.

The Borgia Apartment

Pope Alexander VI Borgia (1492-1503) lived in this apartment, which is situated under the Rooms of Raphael and occupies the first floor of what was the Palace of Nicholas V (1447-1455). It is composed of six rooms. Part of it has almost the structural appearance of a fortress: the first two rooms, the Room of the " Sibyls " and the Room of the " Creed ", are situated within the **Borgia Tower.**

Pinturicchio (1454-1513) painted the apartment with frescoes of *scenes from sacred history and mythology.* He also decorated it with stucco reliefs.

The **Room of the " Sibyls "** comes first. It takes its name from the twelve half-figures of sibyls, each accompanied by a prophet, that look out from the lunettes of the double vault.

The fresco, which is not by the hand of Pinturicchio, is intended to indicate the symbolic link between the Jewish and the pagan world, as they waited together for the coming of the Messiah.

In the **second room,** that of the " **Creed** ", *prophets and apostles* are shown in pairs, to indicate the continuity between the Old Testament and the New. It appears that the paintings are by Antonio da Viterbo, known as Pastura (died 1516), after drawings by Pinturicchio. The name of the room derives from the scrolls bearing the articles of the *Creed* that each of the twelve apostles is holding.

The **third** is the **Room of the " Liberal Arts "** and was Pope Alexander VI's study. The frescoes in the lunettes glorify the

Pinturicchio: The Visit of the Magi

arts and sciences, represented as allegorical female figures on golden thrones. These too seem to have been painted by Pastura. Of note are the paintings in the vault with the arms of the Borgia family, between reliefs in gilt stucco.

The **fourth room** is called the **Room of the " Lives of the Saints "**, with scenes associated with certain saints. It is a masterpiece by Pinturicchio. The most admired frescoes are the *Disputation between Saint Catherine of Alexandria and the Philosophers*, the *Visit of Saint Anthony the Abbot to Saint Paul the Hermit in the Desert*, the *Visitation*, and the *Martyrdom of Saint Sebastian*.

The **fifth room** is that **of the " Mysteries of the Faith "**. It is decorated with large lunettes with frescoed *scenes from the life of Christ and that of Our Lady*, such as the Annunciation, the Nativity, the Epiphany, the Resurrection, the Ascension, Pentecost and the Assumption. Specially noteworthy is the *portrait of Pope Alexander VI* kneeling before the Risen Christ. This is certainly by Pinturicchio.

The **sixth room** is the **Room of the " Popes "**. It is the largest and was once used for solemn audiences. The painting and ornamentation of the imitation vaulted ceiling are by Giovanni da Udine and Perin del Vaga, pupils of Raphael, who carried out the work at the direction of Leo X (1513-1521).

The then customary theme of the signs of the zodiac and the constellations is seen in the stuccoes adorning the room.

The Sistine Chapel

The Sistine Chapel, dedicated to Our Lady Assumed into Heaven, was built by Giovannino dei Dolci after a design by Baccio Pontelli between the years 1475 and 1482, at the orders of Sixtus IV (1471-1484), from whom it takes its name. The Sistine is the official private chapel of the popes. Among the various functions that take place in it are the conclaves for papal elections. The *choir-gallery* and dividing *screen* in marble are by Mino da Fiesole (1431-1484) and other artists of the fifteenth century.

Interior of the Sistine Chapel

Botticelli: Moses and the Sons of Jethro (Sistine Chapel)

Michelangelo's ceiling of the Sistine Chapel

The twelve frescoes—six on each side wall—show scenes from the life of Moses and the life of Christ. The scenes relating to Moses are: The *Journey of Moses to Egypt*, by Perugino (1445-1523), the *Call of Moses*, by Sandro Botticelli (1445-1510), the *Crossing of the Red Sea*, by Cosimo Rosselli (1439-1507), *Moses Receiving the Tables of the Law*, also by Rosselli, the *Punishment of the Sons of Korah*, by Botticelli and finally the *Testament and Death of Moses*, by Luca Signorelli (1441-1523). The scenes of the life of Jesus (on the facing right-hand wall) are: the *Baptism of Christ*, a work signed by Perugino, the *Temptations of Jesus* and the *Cleansing of the Leper*, by Sandro Botticelli, the *Call of the First Disciples*, by Domenico Ghirlandaio (1449-1494), the *Sermon on the Mount*, by Rosselli and by Piero di Cosimo (1461-1521), the *Giving of the Keys*, a masterpiece of Perugino, and the *Last Supper*, also by Cosimo Rosselli.

The vaulted ceiling of the Chapel has frescoes painted by Michelangelo between 1508 and 1512 at the direction of Julius II (1503-1513). They depict scenes from Genesis. Beginning from the altar, they are: *God Separating Light from Darkness*, an ethereal representation of the Creating Spirit; the *Creation of the Sun, Moon and Plant Life;* the *Separation of Land and Sea;* the *Creation of Man* (showing God infusing life into the already formed body of Adam, placing his finger close to Adam's); the *Creation of Woman;* the *Fall* and the *Expulsion from Paradise*, a dramatic composition in the manner of a triptych; *Noah's Sacrifice;* the *Flood*, with scenes of tragic terror in which is clearly shown the human instinct for self-preservation; and finally, the *Drunkenness of Noah* (showing him being mocked by his son).

Each of these pictures on the vault has at its corners four nude figures, who seem to be commenting on the events described in the fresco.

All along the vault, seated on great thrones, are alternating figures of prophets and sibyls. There is a marvellous representation of Jeremiah weeping as he foresees the fate of Jerusalem.

At the corners of the vault are four scenes from the Old Testament: the *Punishment of Haman*, the *Bronze Serpent*, *Judith* (shown cutting off the head of Holofernes), and the *Slaying of Goliath*.

The figure of Christ the Judge
in Michelangelo's Last Judgment
(wall above the altar of the Sistine Chapel)

The **Last Judgment** on the wall behind the altar was painted in the pontificate of Paul III between 1535 and 1541, some thirty years after the frescoes of the vault, when Michelangelo was over sixty years of age.

Critics have observed that, while in the vault Michelangelo depicts the more or less happy beginning of mankind on this earth, in the later work the language of his composition shows a preoccupation with ultimate religious problems more than with art alone. The content counts for more than the form, in complete harmony with Catholic teaching. However, the two elements attain a fusion that cannot easily be put into words.

At the top is depicted Christ as judge in the act of condemning the wicked, whose faces are marked by intense grief and dismay, while the saved manifest inexpressible joy. The scene covers some two hundred square metres and contains more than 390 figures, many of them over two metres tall.

Among the most important figures in this great work are those of Our Lady, Saint John the Baptist, Saint Andrew with his characteristic cross, Saint Peter with the keys of his supreme power, and Saint Paul beside him. At the feet of Christ is Saint Laurence with his gridiron, and beside him Saint Bartholomew bearing his flayed skin, on the folds of which is seen the self-portrait of Michelangelo. On the left of this central group are the holy women. On the right are male figures, among them Simon of Cyrene carrying the Saviour's cross, Dismas, the good thief, with his cross, and also many martyrs, such as Saint Catherine with her wheel, and Saint Sebastian in the act of stretching his bow. On the level below this we see on the left the risen ascending to heaven and the angels blowing trumpets, and on the right the damned being cast down into hell. The figure of the *Soul in Despair* is unforgettable: with one eye he is looking

Raphael, The Fire in the Borgo

down into the abyss, while he covers the other eye with his hand. On the lowest level, the resurrection of the dead is shown on the left; in the centre is a cave full of demons; and on the right is the entrance to hell, with Charon's boat (a clear reference to Dante's Inferno) and Minos, the judge of the lower regions. Michelangelo gave Minos the appearance of Biagio Martinelli da Cesena, Master of Ceremonies of Paul III, adding to the description given by Dante two long ass's ears, because the Master of Ceremonies had dared to criticize his work.

The Last Judgment in the Sistine Chapel is the *Dies Irae* of the twilight of the Renaissance and also the most grandiose manifestation of the Counter-Reformation, so strongly willed by Paul III and brought to realization later by the Council of Trent (1545-1563) which he convened.

The Rooms of Raphael

Towards the end of 1508, Julius II (1503-1513) entrusted to the then twenty-five-year-old Raphael (1483-1520) the painting of his apartment in the Vatican. This is now called the *Rooms of Raphael.* The artist worked here from 1508 to his death.

The **first room,** which was the last to be painted by Raphael (1514-1517) and some of his pupils, presents the dramatic sight of the *Fire of the Borgo.* On that occasion, according to a well-known mediaeval source, Leo IV (847-855) extinguished a violent conflagration in Borgo Santo Spirito in Rome by making the sign of the Cross. The inspiration for the scene comes from Virgil's description of the burning of Troy.

The *Oath of Leo III* (795-816) brings us the scene in the mediaeval basilica of Saint Peter when that Pope spontaneously cleared himself of the calumnies made against him by his enemies.

The critics agree in not attributing to Raphael the *Coronation of Charlemagne,* because of its inferior quality and its hints of an almost manneristic style. In these last two paintings the artist gives Pope Leo III the appearance of Leo X (1513-1521), his patron, while the emperor Charlemagne is made to resemble Francis I (1515-1547).

For love of his old master, Raphael did not interfere with the painting of the vaulted ceiling of the room, which is by Perugino (1445-1523). The theme of the wall paintings was meant to honour Leo X by exalting the work of two of his predecessors of the same name, Leo III and Leo IV.

The **Room of the Signatura,** which comes next, was intended as Julius II's study and private library. Evidence of this is the

Raphael: The School of Athens

choice of themes for the frescoes, which represent the three fundamental ideas of the True, the Good and the Beautiful.

The *Disputation of the Blessed Sacrament* is the first of the great frescoes painted in the Vatican by Raphael. The work could be considered the *glorification of the Catholic Faith which glorifies the Holy Eucharist.* Heaven and earth are united to the Trinity in the central mystery of transubstantiation. The fresco also shows the union of the pilgrim Church with the Church triumphant in heaven.

In the work are found several portraits, including those of Dante, Savonarola, Fra Angelico and Bramante. It should be added that the traditional name of Disputation is in fact inaccurate. The work would be better called the *Triumph of the Church.*

The *School of Athens* shows an imaginary meeting of the most famous philosophers of antiquity. It is presided over by Plato and Aristotle. Here too are various portraits: Diogenes is Leonardo da Vinci, Euclid is Bramante. Beside the latter, on the right, is Raphael himself, and in the foreground is seen the face of Michelangelo in the character of Heraclitus, the pessimist philosopher.

Three cardinal virtues (Fortitude, Prudence, and Temperance) are depicted in bright colours in the lunette on the right of this fresco. They symbolize the moral content of the Law.

Another marvellous creation by Raphael is the fresco of *Parnassus* (1511). On the summit of Mount Parnassus Apollo is playing the lyre in the shade of bay trees. The Muses are grouped around him listening. Among the poets shown in the painting we see Homer, Virgil, Dante and Petrarch.

Below are two scenes in chiaroscuro representing *Augustus preventing the friends of Virgil from burning the Aeneid* and *Alexander placing the poems of Homer in the tomb of Achilles.*

Raphael: The Expulsion of Heliodorus (detail)

On the vaulted ceiling Raphael has painted representations of the sciences and arts. *Theology* is a female figure in a white veil, red dress and green cloak, indicative of the three theological virtues of faith, charity and hope. Then there is *Justice* holding the scales, and *Philosophy*, in whom are symbolized the four elements: in blue, air; in red, fire; in sea-green, water; and in fawn-brown, earth. At the corners of the vault are: the *Fall*, the *Primum Mobile*, the *Judgment of Solomon,* and the *Punishment of Marsyas.* In the fresco there is also a representation of

Poetry, dressed in blue and holding a book in her right hand and a musical instrument in her left. In the pavement are the arms of Nicholas V (1447-1455) and Leo X (1513-1521).

The **Room of " Heliodorus "** was painted between 1512 and 1514. In it are to be seen the new colour combinations adopted by Raphael. The subjects illustrate the miraculous interventions by God to protect the Church.

The *Expulsion of Heliodorus,* with its strong dramatic tones, alludes to the crusade of Julius II against the foreigner in Italy.

On the wall of the entrance is a magnificent painting of *Leo I* (440-461) *halting the invasion of Attila,* an allusion perhaps to the Battle of Ravenna (11 April 1512). Cardinal Giovanni de Medici, the future Leo X, was present at this battle, which led to the departure of the French from Italy. In the foreground Leo I, mounted on a white mule, advances with dignified serenity, followed by two cardinals. His face is a portrait of Leo X.

On the right-hand wall is a painting of the famous *Miracle of Bolsena* (1263), in which drops of blood fell from a consecrated host. This miracle prompted the Bull of Urban IV (11 August 1264) instituting the feast of " Corpus Christi ".

On the remaining wall is the *Deliverance of Saint Peter:* the apostle is brought out of prison by an angel and passes between the sleeping guards. A splendid effect is produced by the moonlight and the radiance coming from the figure of the angel.

The **Room of " Constantine "** was painted by pupils of Raphael after his death in 1520. The name of the room comes from the great frescoes showing the main events in the life of the emperor Constantine, including his baptism and his victory over Maxentius at the Milvian Bridge.

Specially noteworthy is the fresco of the *Vision of the Cross* by Giulio Romano (died in 1546).

Raphael's Loggia

The loggias of the cortile di San Damaso—the second-floor loggia being named after Raphael (1483-1520)—were begun by Bramante at the direction of Julius II in 1512. They were completed by Raphael in 1519, shortly before his death. The ornamentation is the work of Raphael's pupils and based on his designs.

The second-floor loggia was reserved for Leo X, who kept his collection of antiquities there.

The most valuable works are the paintings depicting *events from the Old and New Testaments* in fifty-two panels. The walls are adorned with elaborate stucco decoration in imitation of the

Courtyard of St Damasus,
showing the three Loggias

Raphael's Loggia

Roman models which had been discovered shortly before in the " Domus Aurea ", and which Giovanni da Udine succeeded in reproducing by using a mixture of lime and powdered marble.

The Chapel of Fra Angelico (or of Nicholas V)

It is given this name becáuse, although dedicated to Saint Stephen and Saint Laurence, it was painted by Fra Giovanni da Fiesole, known as Fra Angelico (1400-1455). He carried out this work at the bidding of Nicholas V between the years 1448 and 1450. The frescoes present scenes from the lives of the two holy deacons, while seated figures of the four *Evangelists* are seen among the clouds on the vaulted ceiling, which is painted blue and decorated with stars.

On the pilasters are frescoes of *doctors of the Church,* including Saint John Chrysostom, Saint Gregory, Saint Augustine and Saint Thomas Aquinas.

From the events in the life of Saint Stephen one sees his *disputation with the judges before the Sanhedrin* and his *martyrdom.* Among the scenes of the life of Saint Laurence are the *conferring of the diaconate by Sixtus II* (257-258) (who is given the features of Nicholas V), *Saint Laurence in prison converting his guard,* and his *martyrdom on a gridiron.*

The floor is paved in marble and depicts the sun and the signs of the zodiac.

The very individual style of Fra Angelico and his devout mysticism make this Chapel one of the most precious works of the Renaissance.

The Room of the Immaculate Conception

Between the two floors of the Borgia Tower is the Room of the Immaculate Conception. The frescoes by Podesti (1800-1895) recall the solemn proclamation of the *dogma of the Immaculate Conception* by Pius IX on 8 December 1854.

On the walls, between the windows of the room, are pictured the *Sibyls* prophesying, according to an ancient pious tradition, the divine motherhood of Mary. On medallions in the vaulted ceiling are *scenes from the lives of Esther and Judith* together with allegorical figures representing *Faith* and *Theology.*

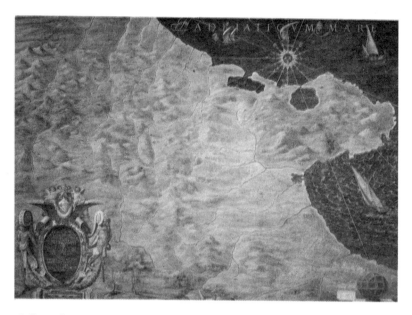

Gallery of Maps:
the Adriatic Region (present-day Apulia)

In the middle of the room is the wooden model of *Saint Peter's Dome,* executed at the direction of Michelangelo between the years 1556 and 1560, with the modifications for the outer shell introduced by G. Della Porta.

The Gallery of Maps

This is a long corridor (120 metres by 6) built by Ottaviano Mascherino under Gregory XIII (1572-1585), who had it painted with maps of the various regions of Italy and the territory of Avignon, which was then a possession of the Apostolic See.

There are also smaller paintings of the Battle of Lepanto, of the Tremiti Islands, and of the harbours of Genoa, Venice and Civitavecchia.

The maps number thirty-two; on the left are the Tyrrhenian regions and on the right the Adriatic ones. On the maps are depicted the most notable historical events which occurred in these areas.

This is the most important cartographical enterprise of the Renaissance. It was carried out between 1580 and 1589 by the geographer Ignazio Danti da Perugia.

Gilded stucco-work and historical or allegorical frescoes adorn the barrel vault, which was painted by Cesare Nebbia and other artists under the direction of Muziano (1528-1592). The frescoes were restored in the time of Urban VIII (1623-1644).

The Tapestry Gallery

At one time the famous tapestries based on designs by Raphael were housed here, but they have since been moved to the Vatican Picture Gallery.

Fifteenth century tapestry made in Tournai,
depicting Episodes of Christ's Passion

Nike

The *New School* tapestries, still kept in the Gallery, were made after the death of Raphael. The cartoons are by his students. In the same Gallery there is also a series on the life of Urban VIII, from the Barberini Works.

The Gallery of the Candelabra

This Gallery takes its name from the fine marble candelabra placed at each of the arches, and is located in the western wing of the Cortile del Belvedere. It was planned by Bramante and built during the pontificates of Pius V and Gregory XIII.

Pius VI had the Gallery decorated according to designs by Simonetti and Camporese. It is about eighty metres long and is divided into six sections. The ceiling vaults were painted by Domenico Torti and Ludovico Seitz (1833-1887) and illustrate events of the pontificate of Leo XIII (1878-1903).

The large candelabra mentioned above were discovered in the seventeenth century near the Basilica of Saint Agnes on Via Nomentana and were placed here by Clement XIV (1769-1774). Each consists of a three-sided base, a stem in the shape of plants or flowers and a very broad basin constituting the actual lampstand. They seem to date from the first or second century A.D.

Worthy of special mention is the statuette of *Nike* (Victory) leaning against a trophy and with her right foot resting on the

The Hall of the Chariot

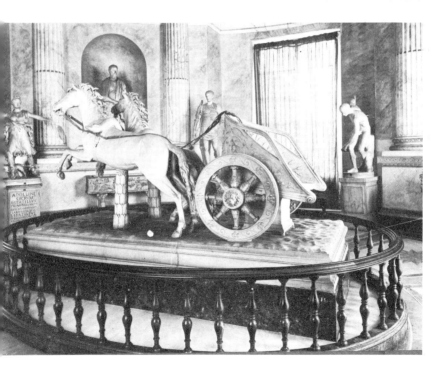

prow of a ship. It is a Roman work of the imperial period after a Greek model of the second century B.C., and probably commemorates a naval victory.

The Hall of the Chariot

Above the *Vestibule of the Four Gates* is the Hall of the Chariot, built at the direction of Pius VI (1775-1799) and designed by Camporese.

In the centre there is a magnificent *biga* or two-horse chariot assembled by Franzoni in 1788. For the frame of the carriage and part of the horse on the right, the only really ancient parts, he used fragments of a work of the first century A.D. The frame had previously been used as an episcopal chair in the Church of Saint Mark in Rome.

The Gregorian Etruscan Museum

Established by Gregory XVI in 1837, this is a collection of objects coming for the most part from the tombs of southern Etruria. Later discoveries in Latium under Pius IX (1846-1878) and a re-organization under Pius XII (1939-1958) made it possible to enrich the Museum with archaeological items which render it famous and unique of its kind.

An outstanding part of the material in the Museum is an imposing collection of Greek vases and a more modest collection of Roman antiquities.

The Museum has eighteen rooms. In the **second room** is material from the famous Regolini-Galassi tomb, brought from

Amphora made by Exechias, showing Achilles and Ajax playing a game of chance

The Mars of Todi

Cerveteri in 1837. The tomb is of the tumulus type, consisting of an access corridor, a chamber at the end and two side recesses. It dates from 650 B.C. and served for three individuals: a man was buried in the central chamber, a woman in the inner room, and the ashes of a cremated man were placed in the right-hand recess, near the entrance.

In front of the steps leading from the **third room,** called the **Room of the Bronzes,** into the next one, the **Room of the Urns,** stands the *Mars of Todi,* a figure in armour of the fourth century B.C. bearing inscriptions on the breastplate in the Umbrian language. It is the most famous work in the Museum.

In the second section of the **twelfth room** is the *Stele of the Athlete,* an Attic sepulchral relief from the middle of the fifth century B.C. It represents a youth with his left arm raised in greeting, while his young slave holds a vase of ointment and a strigil, the instrument with which athletes used to clean their bodies of sweat and dust after the contest. The work succeeds in perfectly representing a lively youth.

The Vatican Picture Gallery

The present building of the Vatican Picture Gallery was erected at the direction of Pius XI (1922-1939). It is the work of the architect Luca Beltrami and is in the Lombard Renaissance style. It was inaugurated on 22 October 1932.

The founding of the first picture gallery, however, goes back to Pius VI (1775-1799). As a result of the Treaty of Tolentino (19 February 1797) the most important paintings in the gallery became the property of France. Fifty-seven out of a total of a hundred and thirty-three were recovered in 1816 as a consequence of the Congress of Vienna, and were returned to their lawful owners on condition that *they should be put on view for the enjoyment of the public.* In conformity with this condition, Pius VIII (1829-1830) opened a Picture Gallery in the Borgia Apartment. It contained forty-four paintings. The Gallery was frequently moved to other parts of the Apostolic Palace in later years, until Pius XI fixed its present site and supplemented the two hundred and seventy works already in the old Gallery with

Giotto: The Stefaneschi Polyptych (reverse)

a further one hundred and eighty-three taken from the Vatican apartments, the Papal Villa at Castelgandolfo and the Sacristy of Saint Peter's. Under Pius XII (1939-1958) the Gallery was further enriched with a section dedicated to contemporary works.

A bust of Pius XI stands in the vestibule.

The **first room** is that of the **Byzantine School and the Italian Primitives,** and is mainly devoted to Byzantine and primitive works. Almost all the icons belong to the sixteenth and seventeenth centuries. The most important works are *Christ Blessing,* a twelfth-century Byzantine painting, and *Saint Francis,* a signed work by Margaritone d'Arezzo (XIII century). To the Roman Benedictine School belongs the *Last Judgment* (XI century); the *Virgin and Four Saints* is by Giovanni Bonsi (XIV century).

In the **second room** are mainly paintings of the fourteenth century, and some of the first part of the fifteenth. Particularly important are the *Redeemer Blessing* by Simone Martini (1285-1344), the *Madonna of the Magnificat* by Bernardo Daddi (XIV century), the *Vision of Saint Thomas Aquinas* and the *Madonna and Child* by Stefano di Giovanni, called " Sassetta " (1392-1450); also the *Miracles of Saint Nicholas* by Gentile da Fabriano (1360-1427).

Also in this room is the *Stefaneschi Polyptych* by Giotto. This work was originally in St Peter's. It shows Christ seated on a throne and surrounded by angels, and the martyrdom of the Apostles Peter and Paul. The artist, freeing himself from the Byzantine style, gives his figures a more vigorous and dramatic aspect. At the feet of Jesus is Cardinal Stefaneschi, the donor of the work. On the reverse is the enthroned figure of St Peter, with the Apostles James and John on either side.

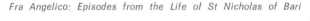

Fra Angelico: Episodes from the Life of St Nicholas of Bari

The **third room** is that **of " Fra Angelico "** (Fra Giovanni da Fiesole, a Dominican: 1400-1455). Here can be seen his *Scenes from the Life of Saint Nicholas of Bari* and the *Virgin and Child between Saint Dominic and Saint Catherine.* The always harmonious figures are painted in luminous colours, with a predominance of red and blue. The *Coronation of the Virgin* is by Fra Filippo

Melozzo da Forlì: Sixtus IV names Bartolomeo Secchi, known as Platina, Prefect of the Vatican Library

Raphael: The Transfiguration

Lippi (1406-1469) and the famous *Madonna of the Girdle* is by Benozzo Gozzoli (1420-1497).

The **fourth room** is that **of " Melozzo da Forlì "** (1438-1494), so called because of the fourteen fragments of his great fresco of the *Ascension of Jesus into Heaven.* This fresco was once in the apse of the Basilica of the Holy Apostles in Rome and is a precious work by this artist. His *Angel Musicians,* seen in this work, are famous for the accuracy with which he painted the musical instruments.

Another large fresco by Melozzo portrays *Sixtus IV naming Bartolomeo Secchi, known as Platina, Prefect of the Vatican Library.* It was put on canvas in the time of Leo XII (1823-1829). Platina, author of the famous Lives of the Popes, is kneeling before the seated Sixtus IV. To the right of the Pope is Raffaele Riario, who is holding the scroll of the nomination. The standing cardinal is the future Julius II, nephew of Sixtus IV.

153

Tapestry after a drawing by Raphael,
The Miraculous Draught of Fishes

In the **fifth and sixth rooms** are works by lesser artists of the fifteenth century. Especially important is the painting of the *Miracles of Saint Vincent Ferrer* by Francesco del Cossa (1435-1477). It is marked by a very effective dramatic intensity, which is well suited to the *Angel of the Judgment,* the name popularly given to the Dominican preacher. The polyptych *Madonna and Child with Saints* is a work by Vittore Crivelli, while that of *Saint Anthony the Abbot with other Saints* is by Antonio Vivarini of the Murano School.

Leonardo da Vinci: Saint Jerome

Titian:
Madonna of San Nicolò dei Frari

155

The **seventh room** is devoted to the Umbrian School of the fifteenth century, including Pietro Vannucci, known as Perugino, and also Pinturicchio. A typical work by Perugino (1445-1523) is the *Virgin Enthroned*, with its very lively colours, perfectly balanced composition and especially graceful outlines. Other small pictures by Perugino depict Saint Benedict, Saint Placid and Saint Flavia. Pinturicchio (1454-1513) was a less elegant painter but a very effective one. His *Coronation of the Virgin* and his *Madonna and Child* are in this room.

The **eighth room,** the. **Room of " Raphael ",** can be called the *shrine* of this artist (1483-1520). It is dominated by large paintings representing the highest points of his art: the *Coronation of the Virgin,* the *Madonna of Foligno* and the *Transfiguration.* This last is his most famous work. It is divided into an upper and a lower part, and succeeds in giving an idea both of the supernatural atmosphere on Mount Tabor, where Jesus is shown transfigured before the Apostles Peter, James and John, and of the ephemeral confused atmosphere of earthly life, where the other Apostles are shown struggling with a possessed man. Of special artistic interest are the tapestries executed after cartoons by Raphael for Leo X (1513-1521) to decorate the walls of the Sistine Chapel. They show the *Miraculous Draught of Fishes* and certain events from the *Acts of the Apostles.*

The **ninth room** is devoted to Leonardo da Vinci (1452-1519). Among the exhibits is his *Saint Jerome,* an unfinished work, but one unmatched for the light which shines on the face of the holy doctor and for its vivid realism.

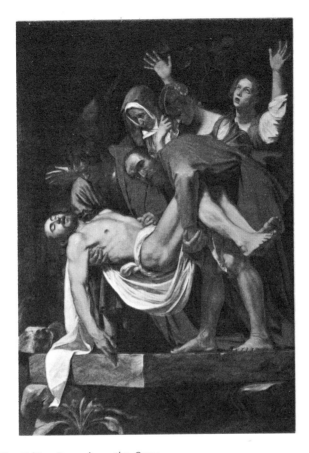

Caravaggio: The Taking Down from the Cross

The **tenth room** contains masterpieces of the Venetian school of painters, the greatest of whom was Tiziano Vecellio (1477-1576), known in English as Titian. On view here is his *Madonna of San Nicolò dei Frari.* Next is a work depicting Saint Helena by Paolo Caliari, known as Veronese (1528-1588). Another work of great artistic worth is the *Saint Bernard* by Sebastiano del Piombo (1485-1547).

The **eleventh room,** the Room of the **" Late Renaissance and Early Baroque ",** houses the painting of the *Madonna of the Cherries* by Barocci (1528-1612). Girolamo Muziano from Brescia (1528-1590) is represented by his *Resurrection of Lazarus,* in which is apparent the influence of the Lombard and Venetian schools. There are also two works showing a reaction to the mannerism of the late sixteenth century: the *Trinity with the Dead Christ* by Annibale Carracci (1560-1609) and the *Sacrifice of Abraham* by Ludovico Carracci (1555-1619).

The **twelfth room,** octagonal in form, is very large and houses works of famous seventeenth century painters. The most notable is Domenico Zampieri, known as Domenichino (1581-1641), with his famous picture of the *Communion of Saint Jerome.* Guido Reni (1575-1642) belongs to the same school; in this room are his paintings of the *Crucifixion of Saint Peter* and the *Virgin in Glory with Saint Thomas and Saint Jerome.* Also in this room is the *Deposition* by Michelangelo Amerighi, known as " Il Caravaggio " (1569?-1610).

In the **thirteenth and fourteenth rooms,** called the Rooms of the **" Seventeenth and Eighteenth Centuries ",** are housed a large picture of *Saint Francis Xavier* by Anthony Van Dyck (1599-1641) and other works by Flemish, French, Italian, Dutch and German artists. Paul Rubens (1577-1640) is represented by his *Triumph of Mars,* and Guido Reni by his *Fortune.*

The **fifteenth room** is that **of the " Portraits ".** The most famous work is the *Doge Niccolò Marcello* by Titian (1477-1576). By Carlo Maratta (1625-1713) there is the *Clement IX Rospigliosi,*

Marsyas

an excellent example of seventeenth-century portraiture. The *portrait of Cardinal Lambertini,* who later became Benedict XIV (1740-1758), is by Giuseppe Maria Crespi (1665-1747).

Three rooms follow, in which there is a collection of contemporary works given to the Gallery by the artists themselves or by private collectors.

The Gregorian Pagan Museum

The Gregorian Pagan Museum contains the works of art that had previously been housed in the Lateran Museum, which was established by Gregory XVI (1831-1846) in the Lateran Palace and opened by him on 14 May 1844. By order of John XXIII (1958-1963) the Museum was transferred to the Vatican. Reopened to visitors in 1970, it contains mainly material discovered in the former Papal States. The principal items are ancient sculptures. Some of these are copies of Greek models of the classical period, while others are original Roman works whose dating varies from the end of the Republic to the period of the Empire. There are also sepulchral altars and sarcophagi, and mosaics from the two great exedrae of the Baths of Caracalla, representing athletes and judges of contests. There is also a large collection of inscriptions.

To the right of the doorway, a marble bust recalls the founder of the Museum, Gregory XVI. Alongside is a bust of Pius IX (1846-1878), founder of the later Pian Christian Museum.

The most important work to be seen in the first part of this collection is a marble copy of the famous bronze group of *Athena and Marsyas:* the original, attributed to Myron of Eleutherai (450 B. C.), has been lost. It seems to have been a votive offering placed in the Acropolis of Athens. Pliny (60 A. D.) and Pausanias (160 A. D.) speak of it. Marsyas, who is given a savage and animal-like appearance, is attracted by the sound of the double flute, and approaches with dancing step to pick up the instrument which Athena has thrown away: but the goddess stops him with a gesture of command.

The Daughter of Niobe

A short distance away is a statue of the Athenian tragic poet *Sophocles* (496-406 B. C.). It was discovered in 1839 at Terracina and is of special importance: Gregory XVI was led to establish the Museum for the sake of providing a fitting setting for it. The poet, represented in the vigour of his maturity, stands with a cloak wrapped about him and gazes intently ahead. The statue is a marble copy of a bronze original which was probably commissioned by Lycurgus (340 B. C.) and placed in the Theatre of Dionysus in Athens.

The *mosaic pavement* which is seen a little farther on, depicting banquet remains scattered in disorder on a white background, is a copy of a famous Hellenistic original described by Pliny (*Nat. Hist.* 36, 184). The work bears the signature of a certain Heraclitus. This Heraclitus, however, is not the famous philosopher of Ephesus, even though the mosaic scene is meant to indicate, in some way, the continuous changing of nature—and change was the fundamental theme of Heraclitus the philosopher.

A colossal statue of *Poseidon* (Neptune) stands with the right foot on the prow of a ship and with a large dolphin for support. The figure of the god of the sea, his head framed by luxuriant locks, conveys an impression of special dignity. The original of the work, perhaps in bronze, is reproduced on Greek silver coins and is thought to be of the fourth century B. C. The dolphin was added by the copyist.

Worthy of special note is the relief of the sorceress *Medea*. Although standing among so many copies, it is perhaps a Greek original dating from the fifth century B. C. It depicts the two daughters of Pelias preparing to murder their father. Medea holds a cup containing magic herbs which she is about to pour into the cauldron prepared by one of the daughters, while the other daughter, who holds a cleaver in her right hand, shows a foreboding of tragedy. They have decided to murder their father at the suggestion of the sorceress, who has promised that he will be brought back to life and completely rejuvenated after his body has been cut into pieces and put into the cauldron.

Next there is a group of powerful *male torsos.* They are copies, made during the Roman empire, of figures of Greek gods or heroes. Also interesting is the statue of the *Daughter of Niobe* about to flee from the avenging arrows of the gods; she is protecting herself with her mantle, which billows in the breeze. This is the work of a neo-Attic artist of the first century B. C.

Next comes a collection of Roman sculptures, including *portraits of several of the Caesars,* among them Tiberius and Claudius.

The relief of the *Arca dei Vicomagistri,* found in the period 1937-1939 in what is today the Apostolic Chancery Building (the ancient Campus Martius), represents a sacrificial procession with consuls, lictors, trumpeters, victims and young ministers: it is from the golden era of Roman sculpture, that is, the time of the Emperor Claudius (40 A. D.).

Further on there are *urns and sepulchral altars* from the first century A. D. and later, and *monumental historical reliefs,* such as the Arrival in Rome of Vespasian: he is being welcomed by

Relief on the Arca dei Vicomagistri

his son Domitian, by the Senate and the people. He is shown bowing to the goddess Rome, enthroned on his left with the Vestal Virgins about her.

Another frieze nearby depicts the *Departure of Domitian* (the face was later altered to that of Nerva); he is shown surrounded by magistrates and lictors.

Of excellent quality are the reliefs on the *Pillar of the Roses:* roses are entwined round a candelabrum, at the top of which two peacocks peck at the buds. The work dates from about 120 A. D.

The *sarcophagi of Heracles, Hippolytus and Selene* are decorated with mythological scenes. Some of the gods or heroes are given the faces of the deceased persons, indicating a yearning for the continuation of this earthly life in another beyond the tomb.

Worthy of note is the front of a large sarcophagus showing the seated figure of an *unidentified philosopher*. His gaze is meditative and he is flanked by two female figures, probably representing Muses. The philosopher has been thought to be possibly the neo-Platonist Plotinus, who died in 270 A. D.

A very original sarcophagus shows the *cultivation and processing of grain*. The relief is divided into parts: in the first is depicted a farmer guiding a plough drawn by a pair of oxen, while another person is harvesting. In the second part there is a cart bringing the grain to the mill and two men turning the stone. At the base there is an oven in which bread in being baked. In the centre a person wearing a toga and holding a scroll is the portrait of the deceased, whose name is inscribed on the lid of the sarcophagus. A Latin couplet, which reproduces a Greek epigram, says that the dead man bids farewell to Hope and to Fortune with whom he can have no more dealings and who can now make fools of other men: tragic irony of ancient pagan thought concerning human destiny, so different from the Gospel message.

The Pian Christian Museum

Founded by Pius IX in 1854, this Museum consists of two sections, the second of which is still being arranged. The part already opened displays architectural, sculptural and mosaic exhibits.

It is worth noting the series of *fragments of sarcophagi*, depicting the birth of the Messiah and the Epiphany; they seem to date from the middle of the fourth century.

The *Sarcophagus with the Crossing of the Red Sea* is one of the chief works preserved here. On the left, Pharaoh, followed by his soldiers in chariots, pursues the People of Israel, who are escaping from Egypt by crossing, with divine help, the waters that close over to drown the Egyptian army.

The large so-called *Theological Sarcophagus* comes from the foundations of the baldacchino in the Basilica of Saint Paul Outside-the-Walls. On the top is God, One and Three, creating man and woman; Christ gives Adam a bundle of ears of corn, to denote the toil which he must undertake because of his rebelliousness; to Eve the Redeemer gives a lamb, to point out the

The « Theological » Sarcophagus

necessity, resulting from sin, of labouring to obtain food and clothing.　Behind the woman is the tree of the knowledge of good and evil.　This sarcophagus also dates from the middle of the fourth century A. D.

The beautiful relief on a sarcophagus coming from the Basilica of Saint Ambrose in Milan represents *Christ* as a young man with flowing hair. Seated on Mount Sinai, with his right hand he makes a gesture of preaching, while in his left he holds an open book. Beside him are the Apostles, of whom Peter and Paul are the closest to the Master.

Next comes another sarcophagus, also of the fourth century A. D., with *biblical scenes* and the busts of a husband and wife, only roughly sketched. It was brought from the Basilica of Saint Paul.

The greatly restored statue of the *Good Shepherd* is a familiar one. With the head turned to the right of the viewer, the young Shepherd with long curly hair is carrying on his shoulders the lamb he has found. It should be noted that this exceptional statue does not seem, from the iconographical point of view, to have been originally a Christian invention: from the seventh century B. C. onwards representations of a shepherd bearing a lamb on his shoulders are frequently met with, even in the pagan world. But in its new context the theme undergoes a radical change: for the pagans the figure represented a worshipper carrying his offering to the gods, but the present statue without a doubt represents the Good Shepherd of whom Jesus speaks in the Gospel parable.

A similar representation of the Good Shepherd is to be seen on another sarcophagus kept here. This was discovered in 1881 on the Via Salaria near the Mausoleum of Licinius.

The same figure appears yet again on another sarcophagus found near the Via Appia Antica. In this example the Good Shepherd is standing between two younger men. Around the sarcophagus are depicted the four seasons and scenes of country life. It is a work of the fourth century A. D.

Especially interesting is the front of a sarcophagus coming from the Basilica of Saint Laurence Outside-the-Walls. It represents Jesus as a youth among the Twelve Apostles. In the foreground are twelve sheep symbolizing the flock of Christ.

The Missionary and Ethnological Museum

The Missionary and Ethnological Museum was set up by Pius XI in 1926 in the Lateran Palace.

The scientific and technical arrangement of the material was planned by the famous ethnologist Father William Schmidt, S.V.D., who undertook the scientific direction of the museum, and carried out principally by his assistants, Father Michael Schulien, S.V.D. and Father Pancratius Maarschalkerweerd, O.F.M. The museum was solemnly inaugurated on 21 December 1927.

The basic nucleus of the museum consists of no less than forty thousand collections and single items from the Missionary Exhibition held in the Holy Year of 1925. These had been generously offered to the Pope by one hundred and eighty-five vicariates apostolic, seventy-one prefectures apostolic, seventy-eight missions, and seventy-four archdioceses, dioceses and prelatures, and with the collaboration of one hundred and sixty-three orders and missionary institutes, thirteen native religious communities, numerous scientific societies and private individuals. The Exhibition contained items from every part of the world in which Catholic missionaries work.

Arranged according to geographical areas, it offered a marvellous picture of the lives and widely differing activities of many non-European peoples in the economic, social and artistic fields, as well as illustrating their various religious beliefs and practices.

Even before the inauguration of the museum, other items and collections were added to this nucleus. The first addition came, on the Pope's instructions, from the store-rooms of the Pontifical Vatican Museums. Another came from the Congregation for the Evangelization of Peoples, which ceded to the Ethnological Museum the remaining collections of the Borgia Museum. In addition to these two donations the Pope authorized the purchase of a number of treasures of Indian art.

After the inauguration other gifts continued to arrive for the Pope from all over the world and were placed by him in the Museum. These donations came to an end with the Second World War and were not resumed until much later, when a valuable collection of Persian carpets from Afghanistan and Bokhara was added. These had been collected locally between the two World Wars by an Italian consul, whose widow presented them to John XXIII.

On 1 February 1963 the Museum was closed to the public and by order of John XXIII transferred to the Palazzo di San Calisto. In the following years a new building for the Lateran Museums was constructed near the Vatican Museums. All the material was transferred from the Palazzo di San Calisto to the new site in the Vatican in the years 1969 and 1970.

The Museum is divided into two parts, called respectively The **Main Gallery** and The **Secondary Gallery.** The first, intended for the general public, contains objects illustrating the history of every non-European country's religions or religious culture. In the Secondary Gallery, intended for specialists, the ethnographic collections are displayed.

The **Main Gallery,** which is about seven hundred metres long, is divided into twenty-five sections. Each section covers either one nation or one cultural region of the non-European world, and in each the historical development of the various forms of religion is illustrated. The following is a list of the individual regions.

1. *China:* sky worship, worship of the dead, ancestor worship, Taoism, Confucianism, Islam, Christianity.
2. *Japan:* Shintoism, Buddhism, Christianity.
3. *Korea:* the Museum's entire Korean collection is housed here.
4. *Tibet and Mongolia:* the Bon-Pö religion, Lamaism.
5. *Indochina:* worship of the dead, ancestor worship, Buddhism, Christianity.
6. *The Indian subcontinent:* primitive religions, Shivaism, Vishnuism, cult instruments, syncretic religions, Buddhism, Islam, Christianity.
8. *Polynesia:* worship of the dead, ancestors and deities, cult instruments, Christianity.
9. *Melanesia:* worship of the dead, ancestors and deities, ceremonial masks, cult instruments, spirit houses, Christianity.
10. *Australia:* worship of the dead, totemism, cult instruments.
11. *North Africa:* Egyptian religion, Christianity, Islam.

12. *Ethiopia:* primitive religions, Coptic Christianity.
13. *Madagascar:* ancestor veneration, magic.
14. *West Africa:* Pantheon of Dahomey, worship of the dead, ancestor worship, deities, ceremonial masks, magic.
15. *Central Africa:* ancestors and deities, ceremonial masks, magic.
16. *East Africa:* ancestor worship, cult instruments, ceremonial masks, magic.
17. *South Africa:* ancestor worship, ceremonial masks, magic.
18. *Christian Africa:* Congolese Crib, statues of Our Lady, other Christian sculptures.
19. *South America:* primitive religions, ceremonial masks, higher religions.
20. *Central America:* primitive religions, higher religions.
21. *Christian America:* including the missal-stand of Christopher Columbus's chaplain.
22. *North America:* ceremonial masks, the Pettrich sculpture collection.
23. *Persia:* Persian majolica ware, some with inscriptions from the Koran.
24. *Near East:* Babylonian religions, Hellenistic-Roman religion, Judaism, Christianity, Islam.
25. *Missionary Synthesis:* sacred art, Christian painting, architecture.

In all, in the Main Gallery about three thousand objects are displayed; these however form only seven to eight per cent of all the material in the Museum. The rest of the collections will be on view in the appropriate sections of the Secondary Gallery.

The Museum also contains a prehistoric collection including material from France, Palestine, North Africa and Mongolia.

The Historical Museum

The Historical Museum, set up and arranged at the wish of Paul VI in 1973, is divided into two sections. The first includes a collection of carriages once belonging to popes or cardinals. In the second is a display of equipment of the now disbanded papal armed forces and the former papal army, together with various pieces of armour previously kept in the Apostolic Palace. In the entrance-hall is a bust of Paul VI, while lining the walls are marble busts of the popes who used the carriages preserved in the museum.

Also in the first section are full-dress and half-dress harnesses, saddles, cushions, travelling bags, shafts and reins. On the walls are pictures of religious ceremonies and journeys undertaken by popes, showing the means of transport used at various periods: horses, cars, trains and aircraft.

In the second section are glass cases containing interesting uniforms and military relics, including a set of jousting armour dating from the second half of the sixteenth century, the armour of the papal guards, figures dressed in the uniforms of the Corps of Noble Guards and of the Corps of Papal Gendarmes, and uniforms of the Palatine Guard and of the army of the Papal States. Also on display are helmets, basinets, morions, steel weapons, arquebuses and firearms, together with papal standards and coats-of-arms.

INDEX

VATICAN POLYGLOT PRESS

Lire 800